This book is dedicated to the
Church of Jesus Christ worldwide.

A NOTE FROM THE AUTHOR

When Jesus answers His disciples' question regarding *"...the coming of the Son of man,"* He makes a statement that seems to be contrary to our understanding of endtime events: *"For as in the days that were before the flood they were eating and drinking, marrying and giving in marriage, until the day that Noe entered into the ark"* (Matthew 24:38). It seems strange that He does not mention the terrible development of sin and wickedness, but simply enumerates the normal day-to-day things people occupy themselves with.

For our day, Jesus does not emphasize the breaking up of families, public exhibition of homosexuality, the horrible murder of the unborn, the AIDS epidemic and frightening increases in illegal drug use. He simply tells us that people will be just the same as they always have been and always will be: they eat, they drink, they marry and give into marriage; they buy and sell, plan and build. But He does reveal one important item, *"And knew not until the flood came, and took them all away...."* They did everything that normal people do, but neglected one thing: They did not go into the saving ark God had provided through Noah. Why, we may ask, did they not go into the ark? Answer: Because they were quite busy with their normal way of life and things were going well for them.

Are things going well for us today? We are no longer threatened by dictatorship, communism or Nazism. "We, the people" are in charge. We are a democracy.

People who are secure in their democratic government do not need to take notice of the Scripture's warning that great destruction will come upon the entire world. Thus, the virtual guarantee of peace and prosperity through democracy is causing more and more people to trust in this system and "...know not..." what the Bible has to say about the endtimes. They are neglecting the most important thing, salvation of the soul.

It is ironic that democracy, the system we so love, cherish, and defend, is the only system that seems to match the endtime political scenario whereby the entire world will be united. Strangely enough, it is not through the force of communism, or some dictatorship, but through the peaceful means of election "by the people, for the people," that the prophesied one world system is being established in our day!

FOREWORD

Democracy! There is no doubt that it is the greatest system of government ever devised by mankind. And, today, something remarkable is happening. Instead of communism sweeping west, as had so long been feared, democracy has swept to the east.

Is this the beginning of a great renaissance of modern civilization, or is it laying the groundwork for the rise of the Antichrist?

For many years, prophetic students envisioned a day when the Antichrist would conquer the world by force. Scenarios that pictured tanks on every street corner and troops forcing citizens into compliance were commonplace. But, a closer look at the Scriptures reveals that, far from being a world order created through force, the Antichrist will sweep into power by the will of the people, by democracy. The Apostle John, writing in the book of Revelation, foresees a time when the entire world will admire, love and even worship the Antichrist! That does not sound like the rise of a tyrant, but of the coronation of hero.

In today's world of powerful media images, slick campaigns and decreasing interest in the core issues facing our nations and the planet, it may be that democracy, as the well-thought-out choice of the people, is facing an unparalleled challenge. In a world where Tonya Harding is better known that former U.S. President Warren Harding, and where sitcom re-runs gain higher ratings than presidential addresses, the possibilities are frightening.

In his book, *How Democracy Will Elect the Antichrist*, Arno Froese examines this largely overlooked fulfillment of Bible prophecy and shows how democracy can fulfill key Bible prophecies in a way that communism never could. But, he goes beyond that and shows how this final kingdom fits with other key components of the endtime system.

I hope that this book will spark a renewed discussion as to the role that democracy, freedom and civil rights may play in establishing the prophesied revived Roman empire.

Peter Lalonde
March, 1997

Contents

1. Why Study the Future 9

2. Understanding Prophecy 23

3. Errors of Interpretation 35

4. Family Conflict in the Middle East 45

5. Israel: The Greatest Endtime Sign 67

6. The Mystery of Iniquity and the Rapture 73

7. Mystery Babylon and Her Power 81

8. Mystery Babylon Identified 97

9. Europe in Prophecy 111

10. How Europe Will Lead the World 133

11. The Arising of Global Unity 149

12. Europe Beyond 2000 165

13. The Fake and the Final Kingdom 179

14. True and False Unity 187

15. How Will the World Become One? 199

16. Doomsday Prophecies 209

17. Democracy: The God of the New Age 217

18. The Time of the Gentiles and Israel 225

19. The Great Tribulation and the Day of the Lord 243

20. Countdown to the Rapture 255

21. The Millennium: Beginning and Ending 267

    Endnotes 285

CHAPTER 1

Why Study the Future?

Summary

Almost one-third of the Holy Scripture has a prophetic character. It therefore bids us to study things that are to come. This chapter shows why true believers in Jesus Christ are waiting for His coming. It also clarifies fundamental differences between believing the prophetic Word with our mind and believing with our heart.

Why Study The Future?

When people ask me, "Why should we study the future?", I usually give them about three or four answers.

First of all, the Old Testament tells us, *"Thus saith the Lord, the Holy One of Israel, and his Maker, Ask me of things to come concerning my sons, and concerning the work of my hands command ye me"* (Isaiah 45:11). God is saying that it is a good thing to ask Him about the future.

Second, in the New Testament we are informed by, *"The Revelation of Jesus Christ, which God gave unto him, to shew unto his servants things which must shortly come to pass; and he sent and signified it by his angel unto his servant John"* (Revelation 1:1). Once again, we are told that knowing the future is God's intention for us.

The third answer is common sense. It is part of human nature to want to know as much as possible about the future so we can be prepared for it.

There is certainly a reason why, at least every hour, most radio stations present a weather forecast. Virtually every newspaper gives us complete, although sometimes inaccurate, weather predictions based on developing weather patterns. It is simple common sense to want to know what to expect.

When we take a trip, we consult a map. At the least, we want to know the distance we will be travelling. And, if we are organized, we will try to find out what to expect when we arrive at our destination.

Most of us go into great detail in planning a journey to another country. Let's assume we're planning a trip to Israel. In order to be properly prepared for the journey, we need to find out when our plane leaves, when it will be arriving in Israel, whether we need a visa or a passport, what the weather is like at the time of year we are travelling, what language is spoken, whether we can use U.S. currency, and whether the electrical power is compatible with our blow dryers and electric shavers. These, and hundreds of other questions, continue to crop up as we get closer to the date of our departure.

Whenever we come across a book or an article in a magazine about our destination, we will read all about it. Over and over, our eyes will scan the pictures and the itinerary on our travel brochure to make sure we have not missed any details. If a program comes on television about the land of Israel, we will probably make it a top priority to watch it. We want to know what to expect!

The Importance of Preparation and Planning

I once read a long article describing the preparation for the Apollo moon mission and the final goal of landing a man on the moon. The article stated that during the process, over 500,000 engineers and technicians, working for about 20,000 corporations and firms, participated in the Apollo mission. Preparation for this undertaking took twenty-five years at a cost of over $25 billion! The end result, besides successfully landing a man on the moon, was the collection of nine hundred pounds of moon rocks for research. This mammoth project was heralded as the greatest undertaking in human history. All of it was the result of planning for the future.

Waiting for the Future

All of the 6 billion people on Earth are essentially living for the future. The little ones are waiting to attend school. Those already in school are yearning to "grow up" and enter high school. Quite often, the next step is college or marriage. Day-in and day-out, everyone continues to work, study, and yearn for the future, for tomorrow, for next year, eagerly expecting great and marvelous things for themselves.

This looking to the future does not stop when people are married and have children. Buying their own house is an important goal and dream for the future for many.

When most of our goals are reached or the years catch up with us, we then prepare for retirement. But even when we reach retirement age, we still look toward the future. We hope to have many years left to enjoy grandchildren, and the fruit of many years of labor.

The Future Is Also The End
But what comes next? Well, finally, at last, comes our ultimate destiny: *"...it is appointed unto men once to die, but after this the judgment"* (Hebrews 9:27). Only those who have made the proper preparations for the future of this truth are wise.

Thus, we come to our fourth and main answer for the question, "Why study the future?" Because the future continues for eternity!

Do you now understand how important it is to study the future? It is by knowing our ultimate destiny that we can be sure of where we will spend eternity. Today is the day to make the necessary preparations for the future. Will it be eternally in the presence of our Savior? Or will it be suffering under eternal damnation?

In one of His parables, the Lord Jesus clearly showed the distinct difference between one and the other. Here is what He said in Matthew 13:38–43, *"The field is the world; the good seed are the children of the kingdom; but the tares are the children of the wicked one; The enemy that sowed them is the devil; the harvest is the end of the world; and the reapers are the angels. As therefore the tares are gathered and burned in the fire; so shall it be in the end of this world. The Son of man shall send forth his angels, and they shall gather out of his kingdom all things that offend, and them which do iniquity;*

"And shall cast them into a furnace of fire: there shall be wailing and gnashing of teeth. Then shall the righteous shine forth as the sun in the kingdom of their Father. Who hath ears to hear, let him hear."

You will either belong to one or the other as a result of your own choosing.

In the last book of the Bible we read more about these two groups of people. To the one, the word is given, "rejoice!" To the other, the word given is "woe!" *"Therefore rejoice, ye heavens, and ye that dwell in them. Woe to the inhabiters of the earth and of the sea! for the devil is come down unto you, having great wrath, because he knoweth that he hath but a short time"* (Revelation 12:12).

It is significant to note here that Satan knows that he has but a short time. In other words, as far as the future is concerned, even Satan knows about it. He knows the Word of God. He knows the prophetic Word. Therefore, he also knows the general timing of fulfillment.

Even the Devils Know Prophecy
When the Lord Jesus demonstrated His Messianic ministry, He was met by two men who were possessed with devils. It is important to understand that where Jesus is, there is truth and light. Thus, darkness is exposed immediately in His presence. Jesus did not have to identify Himself to the devils. Nor was it necessary for Him to do anything special. The devils exposed *themselves*, as we can clearly read in Matthew 8:29, *"...they cried out, saying, What have we to do with thee, Jesus, thou Son of God? art thou come hither to torment us **before** the time?"* [Emphasis mine].

Why did the devils protest? Because they recognized Him as the Son of God, the Savior of the world! They apparently knew the prophetic Word. Unto Him (Jesus) was given all power in heaven and on Earth. They lamented in the form of a question: *"...art thou come hither to torment us **before** the time?"* Thus, the devils knew that Jesus would come and destroy the works of the power of darkness. They were aware that ultimately they would end up in the bottomless pit.

However, they also knew that the time had not yet come.
That's why they asked the question!

The Bottomless Pit

When Jesus returns in great power and glory to Earth and His
feet stand on the Mount of Olives, Satan will be arrested and
placed in confinement for a thousand years. Confined to
where? The bottomless pit! *"And I saw an angel come down
from heaven, having the key of the bottomless pit and a great
chain in his hand. And he laid hold on the dragon, that old serpent, which is the Devil, and Satan, and bound him a thousand
years,*

*"And cast him into the bottomless pit, and shut him up, and
set a seal upon him, that he should deceive the nations no
more, till the thousand years should be fulfilled: and after that
he must be loosed a little season"* (Revelation 20:1–3). The
bottomless pit, however, is not the final destination for Satan
and those whose names are not found in the Book of Life.
Their eternal destination is a much more horrible place. It is
called "The Lake of Fire"!

The Lake of Fire

Let's read this serious Scripture which describes the ultimate
end of all who have refused salvation in Jesus Christ: *"And the
devil that deceived them was cast into the lake of fire and brimstone, where the beast and the false prophet are, and shall be
tormented day and night for ever and ever."*

*"And I saw the dead, small and great, stand before God;
and the books were opened: and another book was opened,
which is the book of life: and the dead were judged out of those
things which were written in the books, according to their
works. And the sea gave up the dead which were in it; and
death and hell delivered up the dead which were in them: and
they were judged every man according to their works.*

"And death and hell were cast into the lake of fire. This is the second death. And whosoever was not found written in the book of life was cast into the lake of fire" (Revelation 20:10; 12–15).These passages should give us an additional incentive to study the future to be sure of knowing our path, our final destination.

Spirit of Prophecy

Why study the future? Because the future is prophecy! In Revelation 19:10 we read, *"...for the testimony of Jesus is the spirit of prophecy."* As students of the Word of God, we need to realize that over 25% of our Bible deals with prophecy, with the future. This being the case, we are compelled to study the future. After all, the prophetic Word is an inseparable part of the Holy Scripture.

It is also important to point out that the Bible is the only truly prophetic Book. You won't find prophecy in the Islamic *Koran*, or in the Hindu *Bagavad Gita*. Neither will you find the prophetic Word in Buddhist *Sanskrit*, which actually teaches that man will ultimately drift into nonexistence.

The Bible, which we believe to be the pure Word of God, boldly proclaims the past, the present and the future, *"Behold, the former things are come to pass, and new things do I declare: before they spring forth I tell you of them"* (Isaiah 42:9).

It is the God of Israel, the only eternal God who testifies, *"Ye are my witnesses, saith the LORD, and my servant whom I have chosen: that ye may know and believe me, and understand that I am he: before me there was no God formed, neither shall there be after me"* (Isaiah 43:10).

Fulfilled Prophecy

When we open up our Bibles to the New Testament, right from the beginning we start to read about the fulfillment of Bible prophecy. Matthew 1:22 says, *"...that it might be fulfilled which was spoken of the Lord by the prophet...."* Matthew 2:15 reads, *"...that it might be fulfilled which was spoken of the Lord by the prophet, saying, Out of Egypt have I called my son."*

Verse 17 states, *"Then was fulfilled that which was spoken by Jeremy the prophet...."* Verse 23: *"...that it might be fulfilled which was spoken by the prophets...."*

The New Testament *repeatedly* proclaims that Jesus is the fulfillment of prophecies proclaimed in the Old Testament. If, therefore, He is the fulfillment as written in the past, and the Savior today, then He must also be the fulfillment of future prophecies!

If we study the future, we are really occupying ourselves with the knowledge of our Lord Jesus Christ. After telling the disciples of the events that were to come, He emphasized, *"Behold, I have told you before"* (Matthew 24:25). In John 14:29, Jesus said, *"And now I have told you before it come to pass, that, when it is come to pass, ye might believe."*

Fulfilled Prophecy Disbelieved?

Having seen that the Bible establishes the importance of fulfilled prophecy, we must also point out that fulfilled prophecy was not always believed.

We know that the Jews, in general, did not believe in Jesus, neither did they believe in the fulfillment of the prophetic Word at that time. Therefore, ultimately, they exclaimed, *"...We have no king but Caesar!"* This was outright disbelief! Why did they not believe? Because they relied on their preconceived ideas, expecting the Messiah to be a military revolutionary who would liberate them from the bondage of Roman occupation. From that point of view, we can understand why they did not accept Jesus as the Messiah. Of course, this rejection of Jesus was also fulfillment of Bible prophecy, because

Isaiah 53:3 reads, *"He is despised and rejected of men...and we esteemed him not."*

Disciples Did Not Believe

There are others who did not believe, and they were Jesus' own disciples! When the fulfillment finally came to pass and Jesus arose victoriously as He said He would, we read in Mark 16:11 and 13, *"And they, when they had heard that he was alive, and had been seen of her, believed not."*

"And they went and told it unto the residue: neither believed they them." Why did they not believe? Because at that time they were not born again of the Spirit of God!

Do you recall what Jesus said to the Pharisee, Nicodemus, a ruler of the Jews? He said, *"...Verily, verily, I say unto thee, Except a man be born again, he cannot see the kingdom of God"* (John 3:3). Once our spiritual eyes are opened, we will see the Kingdom of God and begin to study the future. We will study prophecy and we will want to know more about Jesus, because He IS the future!

Head or Heart Knowledge?

Simply having knowledge of the prophetic Word, however, is not sufficient. Let's see an example in the Bible. It is written in Matthew 2 that certain wise men from the East came to Jerusalem and asked the question, *"...Where is he that is born King of the Jews?"* (verse 2). In verse 3 we are told that, *"When Herod the king had heard these things, he was troubled, and all Jerusalem with him."* Why were they troubled? After all, it was a fulfillment of Old Testament prophecy.

Let me explain. We have to realize that these strangers came to Jerusalem, the very place which God had chosen long before to be the dwelling place for His name. Jerusalem was the center of God's plan, the center of all knowledge, and the center of direct contact with the Creator of heaven and Earth.

Gentiles Acknowledge the God of Israel

Over 500 years before the birth of Jesus, a gentile king, Cyrus of Persia, made this profound statement when addressing the Jews while they were in his captivity, *"Who is there among you of all his people? his God be with him, and let him go up to Jerusalem, which is in Judah, and build the house of the LORD God of Israel, (he is the God,) which is in Jerusalem"* (Ezra 1:3). The knowledge of the existence of the God of Israel was already a recorded fact.

The first gentile world ruler, Nebuchadnezzar, made the following statement after the Jewish prophet, Daniel, described and interpreted the king's dream, *"...Of a truth it is, that your God is a God of gods, and a Lord of kings..."* (Daniel 2:47).

Later, we see this same king establishing a law regarding the God of Israel after Daniel's three friends were saved from the fiery furnace, *"Therefore I make a decree, That every people, nation, and language, which speak any thing amiss against the God of Shadrach, Meshach, and Abednego, shall be cut in pieces, and their houses shall be made a dunghill: because there is no other God that can deliver after this sort"* (Daniel 3:29). Thus, we see that the gentiles and the Jews knew about the true God.

Gentiles Announce the Birth of Christ

When the Messiah was born, the wise men from the East came to Jerusalem seeking Him. They were in the right place, asking the right question, to the right people. Unfortunately, they did not receive an answer right away.

First, the king closely questioned his advisers: The scribes, the intellectuals, and the religious experts of his day. *"And when he had gathered all the chief priests and scribes of the people together, he demanded of them where Christ should be born"* (Matthew 2:4). What was the answer? *"...they said unto him, In Bethlehem of Judaea: for thus it is written by the prophet"* (verse 5). What a stunning statement! These Bible scholars clearly knew where the Messiah, the King of Israel, would be born. They consulted the right source, namely, the prophetic Word, *"...for thus it is written by the prophet."*

Now comes the important question: Did these people in Jerusalem, the learned scholars, the religious intellects, believe the prophetic Word? We can answer this question with both "Yes" and "No." "Yes," because they took the Word of God seriously enough to study it, to read what was written in it, and to come to the conclusion, based on the prophetic Scripture, that the Messiah would be born in Bethlehem.

But, we can also answer with "No." Because they only had the intellectual knowledge of the prophecies of the coming Messiah, they did not have the faith in their hearts to believe. If they had believed with their heart, they certainly would have followed these Wise Men to Bethlehem and worshiped the newborn king. That, however, was not the case. Thus, we can determine that these people did not believe in the Holy Scriptures with their heart, but only with their mind!

It is a tragedy! They lived to see the greatest fulfillment of Bible prophecy ever—the birth of the Messiah—but they did not recognize it! They knew that the prophets of old talked about the coming One who would do mighty deeds. And the prophets even gave them accurate details about the Messiah's death. But it was apparently all in vain. They chose not to recognize the fulfillment of Bible prophecy. They were really not interested in studying the future, or understanding the signs of the time. They were blind to the fact that God was doing a great work in their midst! This attitude toward Jesus continued in Israel and is a reality even to this day!

Two Were Waiting for Jesus
When Jesus' parents took Him to the temple in Jerusalem, do we read of a multitude waiting for Him, praising God?

Only two people are mentioned who were waiting at that moment! First, we are told: *"And, behold, there was a man in Jerusalem, whose name was Simeon; and the same man was just and devout, waiting for the consolation of Israel: and the Holy Ghost was upon him"* (Luke 2:25). That's all: *"...There was a man...."* What was so special about this man, that he alone is mentioned here? He was *"...waiting for the consolation of Israel...."* Are *you* waiting for the coming of Jesus?

There is one other person mentioned, *"And there was one Anna, a prophetess, the daughter of Phanuel, of the tribe of Aser..."* (Luke 2:36). She is the other person who recognized the Messiah, *"And she coming in that instant gave thanks likewise unto the Lord, and spake of him to all them that looked for redemption in Jerusalem"* (verse 38). We must emphasize the last sentence which tells us that she did not publish the news about the Messiah to all people everywhere, but she *"...spake of him to all them that looked for redemption in Jerusalem."*

It should not surprise us, therefore, to hear many theologians and pastors today deliberately refusing to study the prophetic Word. Our message that Jesus is coming soon falls on their deaf ears. Thus, we must refocus the message of Jesus' coming to those who look for Him, and bypass those who are only going through religious motions.

Paul emphasizes, *"So that ye come behind in no gift; waiting for the coming of our Lord Jesus Christ"* (1st Corinthians 1:7). He shows us that waiting for the coming of Jesus is a gift from God. These things go hand in hand. Of Simeon, the waiting one, we read, *"...and the Holy Ghost was upon him."* And Anna was totally dedicated in the service of the Lord. Our understanding of Bible prophecy must be synchronized with our service for the Lord. The closer we serve Him, the more fully we will grasp the spiritual significance of the fulfillment of Bible prophecy!

CHAPTER 2

Understanding Prophecy

Summary

Many people believe that Bible prophecy is too complex to understand, so we should just leave it to the "experts." But prophecy can be easily—perhaps we should say readily—understood when viewed with some common sense. The Bible doesn't say that God gave prophecies only to theologians and Biblical scholars, but *"...unto his servants things which must shortly come to pass..."* (Revelation 1:1). This means that you and I can understand God's prophetic Word, and as I pointed out in chapter 1, God expects us to study it because He is the author of prophecy. Surely, we must want to read His book!

Understanding Prophecy

The parallel existence of the Church of Jesus Christ and the preparation for the Antichrist kingdom on this Earth are standard concepts through which Bible prophecy is understood.

Often, Bible prophecy seems complicated because we fail to take into account the fact that some parts of prophecies have already been fulfilled, but others are to be fulfilled in the future.

For example, when John the Baptist was born, his father uttered specific prophecies, of which portions are unfulfilled to this day: *"...Zacharias was filled with the Holy Ghost, and prophesied, saying, Blessed be the Lord God of Israel; for he hath visited and redeemed his people,*

"And hath raised up an horn of salvation for us in the house of his servant David; As he spake by the mouth of his holy prophets, which have been since the world began:

"That we should be saved from our enemies, and from the hand of all that hate us; To perform the mercy promised to our fathers, and to remember his holy covenant;

"The oath which he sware to our father Abraham, That he would grant unto us, that we being delivered out of the hand of our enemies might serve him without fear,

"In holiness and righteousness before him, all the days of our life. And thou, child, shalt be called the prophet of the Highest: for thou shalt go before the face of the Lord to prepare his ways; To give knowledge of salvation unto his people by the remission of their sins" (Luke 1:67–77).

We notice that many parts of this prophecy were not fulfilled during that time, nor have been fulfilled to this day. Let me give you some examples.

Israel's Enemies

Verse 71 says that Israel will be *"...saved from our enemies, and from the hand of all that hate us."* But this has not been fulfilled to this day. As a matter of fact, antisemitism, as a number of reliable sources reveal, is on the increase. Here are some media reports:

> Antisemitic incidents in the United States jumped by 8% in 1993, fueled by a large rise in assaults and threats, the Anti-Defamation League reported....The survey said that assaults, threats and harassment against individuals and organizations rose by 23% over the previous year....ADL National Director Abraham Foxman said... "We are deeply troubled by this in-your-face antisemitism..."[1]
>
> —Reuters, January 24, 1994

> A German news magazine, *Focus*, reported official figures which showed antisemitic attacks had risen more than 100% in Germany in the first six months of 1994, as compared with the same period the year before. Citing a report by the federal police agency BKA, *Focus* reported that 701 such attacks were perpetrated as compared with 343 in the same period of 1993.
>
> Recently, neo-Nazis have been gathering in East German towns shouting "Sieg Heil!" and "Germany for the Germans!"[2]
>
> —Dispatch From Jerusalem, December 1994, p.2

Another Unfulfilled Prophecy

Israel still doesn't serve God today. The Jews are blind to their Messiah, just as Romans 11:28 states: *"As concerning the gospel, they are enemies for your sakes: but as touching the election, they are beloved for the fathers' sakes."*

The priest Zacharias prophesied, *"That he would grant unto us, that we being delivered out of the hand of our enemies might serve him without fear, In holiness and righteousness before him, all the days of our life"* (Luke 1:74–75).

We know that this part of his prophetic utterance has not been fulfilled to this day. They are definitely not delivered from their enemies, neither are they serving God in holiness and righteousness.

The following verses, however, *were* fulfilled at that time, *"And thou, child, shalt be called the prophet of the Highest: for thou shalt go before the face of the Lord to prepare his ways; To give knowledge of salvation unto his people by the remission of their sins,*

"Through the tender mercy of our God; whereby the dayspring from on high hath visited us, to give light to them that sit in darkness and in the shadow of death, to guide our feet into the way of peace" (Luke 1:76–79). Thus, we can see from these verses that a prophetic utterance is not limited to fulfillment all at once. This prophecy was made almost 2,000 years ago. Part of it was fulfilled, other parts are still waiting for final fulfillment.

Jesus' Messianic Proclamation
Another striking example of a partially fulfilled prophecy, often used by Dr. Wim Malgo, founder of Midnight Call, can be seen in Luke chapter 4. Jesus went to Nazareth and attended the local synagogue on the Sabbath. He read the Scripture for that day, *"And he came to Nazareth, where he had been brought up: and, as his custom was, he went into the synagogue on the sabbath day, and stood up for to read"* (Luke 4:16). Then the rabbi in charge handed him the book and He began to read, *"The Spirit of the Lord is upon me, because he hath anointed me to preach the gospel to the poor; he hath sent me to heal the brokenhearted, to preach deliverance to the captives, and recovering of sight to the blind, to set at liberty them that are bruised, To preach the acceptable year of the Lord.*

"And he closed the book, and he gave it again to the minister, and sat down. And the eyes of all them that were in the synagogue were fastened on him. And he began to say unto them, This day is this scripture fulfilled in your ears" (verses 18–21).

What passage did he quote? Isaiah 61:1–2! Let's see what Isaiah wrote, *"The Spirit of the Lord GOD is upon me; because the LORD hath anointed me to preach good tidings unto the meek; he hath sent me to bind up the brokenhearted, to proclaim liberty to the captives, and the opening of the prison to them that are bound;*

"To proclaim the acceptable year of the LORD, and the day of vengeance of our God; to comfort all that mourn."

We notice a distinct difference here. Isaiah proclaimed this utterance in one breath, *"To proclaim the acceptable year of the LORD, and the day of vengeance of our God...."* But in the synagogue on that Sabbath day, Jesus did not read the last part of that verse. He simply stopped after saying, *"...to preach the acceptable year of the Lord...."* He closed the book, gave it to the rabbi and sat down.

Then He said something extremely significant, *"...this day is this Scripture fulfilled in your ears."* The Lord Jesus came to proclaim salvation. He came to fulfill that which was written of Him by the prophets. But He did not come to execute *"...the day of vengeance of our God..."* at that time. That is yet to come.

The prophetic utterance of Isaiah sees the first and second coming of Jesus as one. The 2,000 or so years hidden in between — *"...the acceptable year of the Lord..."* and *"...the day of vengeance of our God..."* — is the time of the church. Only after the church has departed to meet Jesus, *"...in the clouds..."* will the *"...day of vengeance..."* begin.

Fear of the Unknown
By simply recognizing that the prophecies I have cited have only been partially fulfilled, makes their meaning more clear. They start to make more sense. As believers, we have no reason to fear, but God has clearly told us in His Word that those who persist in unbelief will have alot of reasons to fear!

Because of a fear of the unknown, many are reluctant, even deliberately avoid attempting to understand prophecy. Ignoring the prophetic Word, however, does not stop its fulfillment. Those who reject the prophetic Word, or choose to ignore it, cannot be informed of, or properly prepared for that which is to come. Without a clear understanding of the prophetic Word, we would have every reason to fear those things coming upon the world. Here are just a few examples:

Despite recent improvements in the health of our much brooded-over environment, psychologists, sociologists and epidemiologists say we may well be the most anxious, frightened society in our history. Why are we so scared—and so often scared of the wrong things? Many say the news media is largely to blame. The media, after all, pays the most attention to those substances, issues and situations that most frighten their readers and viewers. Thus, almost every day, we read, see and hear about a new purported threat to our health and safety.[3]

—The State, December 25, 1994, p. D1

While we may admit that the world has legitimate reason to fear the things that are happening, Christians have no need to fear. We will only be overtaken by fear if we don't study the prophetic Word.

The Apostle Peter gives us the proper advice, which if heeded, will not lead us into the fear of the unknown, but rather, will make our hearts rejoice: *"We have also a more sure word of prophecy; whereunto ye do well that ye take heed, as unto a light that shineth in a dark place, until the day dawn, and the day star arise in your hearts"* (2nd Peter 1:19). To be fearful of the unknown is not a justification for neglect. On the contrary, if a person ignores the prophetic Word, he will suffer needless fear and miss out on the unparalleled joy that comes with being fully immersed in the Word of God!

The Wrong Place At The Wrong Time

When we devote ourselves to the truth of the prophetic Word, we are in the right place all the time. It gives us the absolute assurance of things to come. But, when we disbelieve the prophetic Word, or ignore it, then we are in foreign territory and are overwhelmed with fear.

Permit me to recall a harrowing experience I had as a young man in Melbourne, Australia.

On this occasion, nightfall came much too quickly. It seemed as if the day just plunged into sudden darkness. What was even more strange and frightening was the almost deadly silence which gave me and my friend, Dieter Fromm, an eerie feeling that something was wrong.

"This can't be happening. This must be a bad dream. It will end instantly the moment we wake up," I thought. But it was much too real. Here we were, two 19-year-old immigrants from Germany, with no knowledge of the English language except a few sentences we had learned on board an Italian immigrant ship named *Castel Felicia*.

The ship laboriously sailed five weeks from Germany to Melbourne, Australia. One particular English sentence stuck in my mind, only because I thought it was so silly, "This is an apple."

I realized you can't walk the streets of the big city of Melbourne with only the knowledge of these four English words and expect to communicate sufficiently to find a place to stay for the night, much less a job. That was the purpose for us hitchhiking to Melbourne, leaving behind the secure immigration camp some 150 miles away. Of course, we were warned at the Bonnegilla camp not to leave the compound.

We were told "The government will take care of you. You will get a job, learn the language, and make money." It was extremely difficult for us to be comforted by such promises because jobs back in Germany were plentifully available.

One could tell their boss, "I quit!" and walk across the street to be eagerly accepted by another firm. Therefore, the warnings not to strike out on our own seemed meaningless to us.

Because we did not heed these words of warning, we found ourselves in an awkward situation many miles away from the camp.

We thought something strange must have happened in the city because it seemed deserted. Never could we have imagined that it was quite normal for an Australian city to be virtually empty after business hours. In Europe, people live in the city, in apartments above stores and offices. But downtown Melbourne was strictly business. When closing time came, everyone went home to the suburbs, leaving the city empty. Thus, the strange and frightening silence contributed to our desperate feeling. A city without people was totally beyond our imagination. "What now?" we asked ourselves. We were lost, hungry, and had virtually no money. Besides, we were in desperate need of a place to sleep. Suddenly, in the darkness of this strange city, we noticed an apparently vacant building. Luckily, the door was left open. Except for some frightened rats running in all directions, we felt rather secure, even elated after closing the door. It seemed a little warmer than outside on the dark street.

Among the trash, we detected a stack of old newspapers, and after eating our last candy bar, the papers became our blankets for the night. "Tomorrow the world will look different," we thought. "We will surely find a job at one of the construction sites and things will improve." We then fell asleep.

It must have been between 2 or 3 a.m. when the cold woke us up. No problem. We knew that heat rises, so we climbed the partially broken wooden stairs to the next floor, bringing with us our paper blankets. We fell back to sleep.

Not long after that, however, we were awakened by the sound of a car, a sound we had so desperately missed during the previous evening. Strangely, the motor stopped, and a car door opened and closed right in front of our building.

We jumped up, looking through the dirty window. My friend recognized a sports car, a British MG. Our hearts really began beating faster when the door downstairs was opened and someone walked in. Almost instantly, I searched for any object suitable for defense and so did my friend. Now, we believed our lives were really at stake.

Thoughts sped through my mind of the many times in my young life that I had just barely escaped death. One time in 1944, for example, our entire family nearly starved because of a Russian curfew. But we came through, losing only one—my youngest sister.

Another time, Germans were being executed at random by the victorious communist forces. But they stopped killing just short of the place where we were staying. So, at this point I was now prepared for virtually anything. But the minutes felt like an eternity.

We clearly heard each footstep and waited in suspense for the sounds to come upstairs. Silence—then the sound of crumpling newspaper. It seemed that the paper was thrown in the direction of the stairs. The suspense was so great that we could hear our own heartbeat.

We did not miss the sound of a striking match. Suddenly it became clear that this fellow was not after us! He didn't even know anyone else was in the building. He probably was an arsonist! Maybe the owner of the building wanted it burned down to collect insurance money.

But, what about us? Should we try to stop him? If he had a gun, we would stand no chance. We could be easily silenced— two witnesses conveniently disappearing in the fire.

We began to smell smoke. Now our desperation grew. If we did nothing, we would die. But if we did something, we still might die. Then the long silence was broken by the sound of footsteps. The door closed downstairs. What an immense relief that was for us. Now we were free to act. Dieter quickly jumped to the window for a glance at a man who hastily jumped into his car through the open roof. He didn't use the door. The engine revved up and the car sped out of sight.

By the time I reached the ground floor, the fire had started on the dry wood of the stairs. Our next decision took only seconds…we extinguished the fire.

Exhausted, we finally walked the sidewalks of this strange city, just happy to be alive. Certainly the arsonist must have been waiting for the smoke and the fire alarm, but in vain, at least this night.

We had considered letting the fire burn, but our presence in the city would perhaps leave us open to suspicion. Any law enforcement officer could immediately identify us as the arsonists because, we were, after all, in the building. Two young men, in a place where they were not supposed to be, speaking virtually no English, having no money, and it would be assumed that we started a fire to keep warm, and that fire had gotten out of hand. That would have been the logical assumption. Happy with our decisions, we were now filled with hope for the new day dawning.

Lost in Foreign Territory

Why am I writing this experience in a chapter dealing with the subject of "Understanding Prophecy"? I do this very purposefully to demonstrate that we were in the wrong place, at the wrong time, getting ourselves into an extremely dangerous situation, because we were navigating territory we had no business being in.

And in just the same manner, this example should serve to remind us that anyone without Christ is totally lost, on their way to eternal damnation. The Bible states that separation from God is forever for those who die without Christ.

If Dieter and I had only known the language, we could have asked someone where we could find a place to stay. We could have easily avoided the terrible situation we had gotten ourselves into.

This experience applies equally to everyone who fails to heed the prophetic Word. They walk in darkness and are oppressed by a terrible fear which need not be.

Eternal Security in Christ

Listen to the guarantee the precious Word of God gives, *"Let not your heart be troubled: ye believe in God, believe also in me. In my Father's house are many mansions: if it were not so, I would have told you. I go to prepare a place for you.*

"And if I go and prepare a place for you, I will come again, and receive you unto myself; that where I am, there ye may be also. And whither I go ye know, and the way ye know" (John 14:1–4).

This is not some kind of cheap advertising, a promotional pamphlet, or well-thought-out "Madison Avenue" propaganda. This is a promise from the living Jesus who made heaven and Earth and everything that is therein!

Are you a child of God? Then you need not fear. Read the book of Revelation which God has given to you detailing the future.

In fact, God gives you a wonderful promise if you read this book: *"Blessed is he that readeth, and they that hear the words of this prophecy, and keep those things which are written therein: for the time is at hand"* (Revelation 1:3).

The study of the prophetic Word, therefore, is not a light thing. Nor is it something that should be left to the specialists. It is for every child of God.

The prophetic Word is an assurance of things to come and it provides us with the hope and comfort that Jesus could indeed come today!

CHAPTER 3

Errors of Interpretation

Summary

As you read this chapter, you will understand some of the false interpretations of prophecies which were popularized after the famous "Six Day War" in the Middle East in 1967. The analysis given in this chapter should also lay to rest the rumors surrounding the "beast computer" in Belgium, the miraculous multiplying of vultures, the continuous claims of discovery of the Ark of the Covenant and other sensational archaeological finds, as well as the adventurous claims of the discovery of Noah's Ark. Such things are not helpful, but only contribute to the growing confusion in today's world.

Errors Of Interpretation

God's Word tells us that to understand Jesus is to understand prophecy. For example, Revelation 19:10 states, *"And I fell at his feet to worship him. And he said unto me, See thou do it not: I am thy fellowservant, and of thy brethren that have the testimony of Jesus: worship God: for the testimony of Jesus is the spirit of prophecy."* Let me highlight the last sentence again, *"...for the testimony of Jesus is the spirit of prophecy."* This is an overwhelming announcement that comes directly from heaven and bears witness once again to the Trinity of the Godhead.

In unmistakable terms, the perfect unity of God the Father, God the Son and God the Spirit in conjunction with prophecy are demonstrated for us here.

Jesus is truth, the Spirit is truth, prophecy is truth. Therefore, when we are dealing with the prophetic Word, we must fully realize that we are dealing with the God of prophecy, with Jesus, and the Spirit of truth!

The testimony of Jesus Christ is truth, whether we choose to believe it or not. Our disbelief, or misinterpretation, does not change the truth.

One Way to Salvation

No one can be saved, but through Jesus. God's Word tells us He is the way, He is the truth, He is life, and no one cometh unto the Father but by Him. This testimony of Jesus Christ is true for all of mankind—past, present, and future. The blood of the Lamb of God is the only substance that cleanses a sinner completely and perfectly, allowing him to stand guiltless in the presence of God the Creator.

We may freely interpret endtime signs the Holy Scriptures give us, but our interpretation must never be considered the final one. We should let the Scripture confirm the Scripture, just as the Lord Jesus and His apostles did.

The Bible is absolute and must be believed literally. When we fail to do this, confusion arises. For example, consider the following news item which was found in the January 3, 1994 edition of *The Scotsman*:

> A fresh dispute over Bible stories has split the Church of Scotland after the moderator described the virgin birth as a symbolic event and attacked religious conservatives. Preaching in Edinburgh, the Rt. Rev. Dr. James Weatherhead, Moderator of the General Assembly, defended controversial doubts recently voiced by church figures, including the Bishop of Durham, over the factual reality of the virgin birth. Dr. Weatherhead, speaking at St. Giles' Cathedral, said the Bible was much more a poetic document than one with legal or literal truths. "We are not necessarily saying anything derogatory at all about the virgin birth if we say it is a symbol," he said.[4]

In this case we see a prominent theologian becoming a fool by denying the literal truth of the Bible and claiming that the virgin birth is merely *symbolic*.

The Church is the Recipient of Prophecy
The Apostle Peter admonishes believers to take heed of the prophetic Word and emphasizes that it is absolutely reliable. He makes a significant statement in 2nd Peter 1:20, *"Knowing this first, that no prophecy of the scripture is of any private interpretation."* The prophetic Word is given to the Church of Jesus Christ, the entire body of believers.

It is, therefore, not left to individual and private interpretation. When an individual believes he has recognized a special truth in the Scripture, he should carefully compare his belief with other men of God and take notice of how they interpret the same Scripture. For example, it is the Spirit of prophecy which emphasizes in these endtimes to so many servants of

God that the time of the gentiles is coming to an end. The church collectively, worldwide, has received this knowledge. It was not a special revelation given to one certain person to recognize it as fact.

The Apostle Peter, who, as we've already determined, rejected private interpretation of the Scripture, emphasized that the Word of prophecy is inspired by God the Holy Spirit. It did not come about by men, *"For the prophecy came not in old time by the will of man: but holy men of God spake as they were moved by the Holy Ghost"* (2nd Peter 1:21).

Prophecies About Jerusalem

Let's look at some prophecies which are being emphasized by the body of believers in Christ today. The fact that Jerusalem, for example, is becoming increasingly a burdensome stone for the nations is a recognized prophetic fact. Such understanding does not need special interpretation. The prophecy is open for all believers. The following example should be recognized as being part of the process leading up to the fulfillment of the prophecy regarding the Holy City.

> Jerusalem should be the peaceful meeting place for...all the children of Abraham, Arabs and Jews alike. But there can be no sovereignty over Jerusalem's holy sites except by the Almighty. I've suggested that a learned group representing all schools within the Islamic world enter an interfaith dialogue with the Christian and Jewish worlds to seek a formula preserving rights and protecting the holy places for all three great monotheistic religions. But I've never suggested that Jerusalem be divided.[5]
>
> —Jordan's King Hussein, U.S.News, November 8, 1993

The King of Jordan is thus seemingly a spokesman for ecumenism between Jews, Arabs, and Christians!

On the other hand, we hear other voices—Arab
Palestinians—quoted in an article in *The Jerusalem Post
International Edition*, June 17, 1995, on page 4:

> About 10,000 members of the Islamic Movement attended a
> "Jerusalem First" rally in Kafar Kassem to demand that east-
> ern Jerusalem be made the capital of a Palestinian state. 'The
> Israeli government and the Likud have agreed on a fact, agree-
> ing that there are two peoples here who share one homeland,
> and each people must be given its own independent state,' said
> Abdullah Nimr Darwish, the head of the Islamic Movement.
> 'This is why we say that Jerusalem's status cannot be harmed.
> Jerusalem first must be, as far as the Palestinian nation is con-
> cerned, the capital of the Palestinian state that will emerge,' he
> said.[6]

As far as the nations of the world are concerned, we know that
virtually all have established their embassies in Tel Aviv, rather
than in Jerusalem, the capital of the Jewish state. Why?
Because they believe Jerusalem should be an international city,
not the capital of a Jewish state. The Bible clearly predicts that
Jerusalem will become the *center* of controversy in the endtimes, thus we know we are approaching the final stages of the
last days.

Prophecies About the State of Israel

We should also all realize that with the reestablishment of the
State of Israel, God began to do a new thing. Therefore, the day
of the completion of the church from among the gentiles can't
be far off.

The reason I say this is based on the fact that the church and
Israel cannot exist side-by-side for an extended period. When
the church began, Israel was being dispersed. Now, Israel is
being regathered so the church must be removed.

Hundreds of thousands, if not millions, of God's servants agree that this is the truth. We are in the last stages of the end-times because of the visible fulfillment of Bible prophecy with the nation and land of Israel. There is too much prophetic evidence to ignore that Israel, even in her state of unbelief, is fulfillment of Bible prophecy.

I will not go into detail here, but it is enough to say that Israel, according to Ezekiel chapter 36, will come back in unbelief, the land that was once a desert will be productive again, and the dispersed shall return and be multiplied in the land of Israel.

These are undeniable facts which we will deal with later in this book.

Sensationalism: A Stumbling Stone In Prophecy

Let us now look at the dangers of misinterpretation and rumor.

During the 1967 Six Day War, Israel captured the entire Sinai Peninsula up to the Suez Canal from Egypt, and took all of the Golan Heights in the north from Syria. Israel was also successful in taking possession of Judea and Samaria. But the greatest prize for Israel was the liberation of eastern Jerusalem. Thus, the city was united once again.

Temple Stones

After the Jews celebrated their victory at the beloved *Wailing Wall*, the last remnant of the western retaining wall of the temple mount where the glorious Jewish temple once stood, rumors began to circulate that Israel was planning to rebuild the new Jewish temple.

Articles appeared in Christian publications alleging that the stones for the temple were cut and ready to be shipped to Israel at any given time. Reportedly, the temple stones were cut in a rock quarry in Bedford, Indiana. After some research, the story was found to be a rumor.

The comments from Israel were, "Stones are the last thing we need. If we could export ours, we could be the richest country on the face of the Earth."

Nevertheless, the temple will be built in due time. Even today, there are a number of Jewish groups such as the *Temple Mount Faithful* who do everything in their power to strive for the building of the temple on Mount Moriah. *The Temple Mount Institute* is preparing temple utensils and training young men as priests in accordance with the Levitical law, so when the temple is built, there will be trained priests to handle the services.

Vultures Multiplying Miraculously

Another sensational rumor that had cropped up revolves around the expected invasion of Israel by a northern confederacy as described in Ezekiel 38 and 39. Verse 17 of chapter 39 reads, *"And, thou son of man, thus saith the Lord GOD; Speak unto every feathered fowl, and to every beast of the field, Assemble yourselves, and come; gather yourselves on every side to my sacrifice that I do sacrifice for you, even a great sacrifice upon the mountains of Israel, that ye may eat flesh, and drink blood."*

An extensive article was published claiming that vultures in Israel were multiplying in unusual numbers. The writer of the article speculated that it was in preparation for the great sacrifice mentioned in verse 17 of Ezekiel 39. The society for the protection of nature in Israel, however, found no evidence to back the reported increase in the number of vultures.

In this case too, we must mention, however, that birds in general are on the increase in Israel, which is mainly due to the revegetation of the land and the innumerable fish ponds that have been built for fish farms. One article in *The Jerusalem Report* stated that Israel has lost more planes due to accidents with birds than they lost during the wars against the Arabs!

The Beast Computer In Belgium

At the European Commission's headquarters in Brussels, another story proclaimed there was a giant 2–story computer, capable of storing information on every person on the face of the Earth. The computer was affectionately called "The Beast." This rumor was reported back in the 70's when Europe was five to ten years behind America in computer technology. This story, too, was later exposed as a hoax.

Noah's Ark and Archeological Artifacts

There have been articles written and videos and movies produced about the discovery of Noah's Ark, the Ark of the Covenant, the gravestones of Mary, Joseph, and many apostles, as well as many other supposed great archaeological discoveries. One sensational discovery seems to be outdone by the next one. But every one of them, when carefully investigated, lacks any factual basis. That, of course, is not to say that there have not been any interesting archaeological discoveries made in Israel.

Whether it is the search for the ashes of the red heifer, the discovery of oil in the tribal territory of Asher, or a supposed geological rift that already exists in the Mount of Olives, these exciting stories rekindle interest. But they are generally not based on facts, rather, they are the product of someone's imagination!

The coming of our Lord does not depend on a rift that supposedly already exists in the Mount of Olives, the discovery of the ashes of the red heifer; the finding of the Ark of the Covenant, neither the excavation of Noah's Ark, or anything else of such nature.

Any visible discovery, whatever it may be, is totally and absolutely insignificant when compared to the Holy Scriptures, which are eternal truth. Only the Bible is unquestionably reliable. We do not need a new discovery to validate it. The full counsel of God is in our possession in the 66 books of our Bible! It is Scripture backed by Scripture that provides all the validation necessary.

What We REALLY Need to Watch

To summarize, let me say this: We need to watch for all reports that speak about the resurrection of Israel, their desperate fight for peace, and the urgency of becoming part of the European Union.

Israel has become a nation: That's prophesied. The Jews are coming back from virtually all nations of the world to that little land: That's prophesied. They will be very successful, although threatened by enemies, and peace will ultimately be negotiated: That too, is prophesied.

And finally, they will accept the false messiah which Jesus prophesied about with the words, *"...if another shall come in his own name, him ye will receive"* (John 5:43). But, rumors will only detour us from our serious exposition of the prophetic Word and we must reject them.

CHAPTER 4

Family Conflict in the Middle East

Summary

Abraham is called the Father of all believers. But only through Isaac, Jacob and his descendants did God promise to fulfill His intention of establishing the Kingdom of God on Earth and offer salvation to mankind. In a compact manner, this chapter shows how Abraham's mistakes brought about the great conflict that is being experienced in our day in Israel and the Middle East: Abraham is also claimed to be the father of the Arabs.

Family Conflict In The Mideast

This century will be known as the most turbulent century in man's history. During the first 45 years, there were two World Wars in which millions upon millions of people perished. It was in this century that communism began to flourish in Russia and spread around the world. But in this century, we also saw the internal collapse of communism, vividly highlighted by the dismantling of the Berlin Wall.

Furthermore, in this century we saw the rise of a sinister spirit that deceived people by attempting to solve the world's so-called Jewish problem. The same spirit was responsible for the rise of the most dreaded antisemitic power structure the world has known. Over 6 million Jews perished at the hands of Germany's murderous Nazi regime under the leadership of Adolf Hitler.

The Return of the Jews

But in this century we also experienced something that is absolutely unique: The return of the Jews to the land of their fathers. It was at the turn of the 19th century when the first Jewish settlers came to the land. They united with those who were already there and began to cultivate parts of the territory called Palestine. Their aim was to revive the land, to bring it back to life, and to produce food for the people that were yet to come.

In the early days, it looked hopeless. But, the Jews persisted and the fruit of their labor was the eventual founding of the State of Israel on May 14th, 1948. Since that time, the focus of attention has shifted dramatically from the new world, the U.S.A., to the old world, the Middle East, as the center of the future.

Parallel to the development of modern Zionism, with its aim to return Jews to the land of Zion, was the phenomenal explosion in the significance of the Arab nations.

Suddenly and unexpectedly, the industrial world saw itself at the mercy of Arab nations who controlled vast resources of oil. While hundreds of books have been written about the Mideast conflict and an almost inexhaustible volume of documentation is available, we want to point out in this chapter that the entire conflict is not merely a political, religious, military, or economic one, but in reality, it is a *family* conflict. Just as two children in a family will fight over one toy, Jews and Arabs continue to fight about the inheritance: The land of Israel.

Abraham: The Beginning of Israel and the Arabs

The man with whom this Arab/Jewish conflict began is Abraham. He was a very unique person because he received a very special promise from God the Creator.

We read in chapter 11 of Genesis about the unsuccessful attempt at world unity through the building of the Tower of Babel, which was supposed to reach up to heaven. Then, in Genesis 12, we read, *"Now the LORD had said unto Abram, Get thee out of thy country, and from thy kindred, and from thy father's house, unto a land that I will shew thee: And I will make of thee a great nation, and I will bless thee, and make thy name great; and thou shalt be a blessing:*

"And I will bless them that bless thee, and curse him that curseth thee: and in thee shall all families of the earth be blessed" (Genesis 12:1–3).

This is not some kind of pronouncement of blessing by a priest, a prophet, or some great dignitary. This blessing was confirmed by the four-fold "I will" given to Abraham by no one other than the Creator of heaven and Earth, the eternal God who always was, who is, and who always will be!

This man, Abraham, was instructed by God to leave everything behind and take a Holy Land journey. He had to leave his country, his kinfolks, even his father's house, and travel to a place yet unknown to him. But this man trusted the living God who had spoken to Him.

One of the unique characteristics of Abraham was that he did what he was told to do. He believed God and immediately acted. For that reason, we read in the New Testament: *"...that he* [Abraham] *might be the father of all them that believe..."* (Romans 4:11).

Abraham was a wonderful, faithful servant of the Lord. He believed in God more than in anything else. Nevertheless, in some instances, he permitted his flesh to run parallel to his faith-life.

Thus the conflict that we see in the Middle East today can be traced back to this great patriarch of the people of Israel and the Arabs.

Abraham and the Arabs

It was Sarai, Abraham's wife, whose patience ran out first. *"And Sarai said unto Abram, Behold now, the LORD hath restrained me from bearing: I pray thee, go in unto my maid; it may be that I may obtain children by her. And Abram hearkened to the voice of Sarai"* (Genesis 16:2).

Abraham, who was 86 years old, had a weak moment. He forgot about his God, and logically came to the point where he, too, must have thought, "We've got to do something!"

It may well have been that he agreed with Sarai, and thought this to be the way of the Lord, thus, he followed the advice of his wife.

"And he went in unto Hagar, and she conceived: and when she saw that she had conceived, her mistress was despised in her eyes" (verse 4).

Obviously, this was *not* God's way. Immediately the problems began. Sarai was now despised in the eyes of her handmaiden Hagar, who bore Abraham a son, his firstborn, who was named Ishmael.

Whether Abraham and Sarah realized that what they had done was wrong is not evident from the Scripture.

Thirteen years later, however, the Lord spoke to Abram, now 99 years old, again repeating the promise He had made to him years before.

But now God changed his name from Abram to Abraham. Abram means "father of height" or "high father," and Abraham means "father of a multitude."

Abraham's Prayer for the Arabs

After receiving additional instructions, Abraham apparently began to think that God was confirming *Ishmael* as His chosen seed. He prayed, *"...O that Ishmael might live before thee!"* (Genesis 17:18).

But God quickly corrected him: *"...Sarah thy wife shall bear thee a son indeed; and thou shalt call his name Isaac: and I will establish my covenant with him for an everlasting covenant, and with his seed after him"* (verse 19).

Nevertheless, God stated very specifically that He had heard Abraham's prayer for Ishmael, *"And as for Ishmael, I have heard thee: Behold, I have blessed him, and will make him fruitful, and will multiply him exceedingly; twelve princes shall he beget, and I will make him a great nation"* (verse 20). However, he emphasized that Ishmael was *not* the covenant bearer, but Isaac *was, "But my covenant will I establish with Isaac, which Sarah shall bear unto thee at this set time in the next year"* (verse 21).

Blessings of Ishmael

The choosing of Isaac, however, did not diminish the tremendous blessing upon Ishmael. Ishmael was to be blessed, to be fruitful, to multiply, not only in a normal manner, but "exceedingly." He was to be the father of twelve princes and not only become a nation, but "a great nation."

The fulfillment of this promise is found in Genesis 25. We read in the genealogy of Ishmael that indeed twelve princes came forth.

Ishmael, therefore, is not to be belittled or rejected, for God gave him and his descendants tremendous blessings and promises as we have just noted.

Nevertheless, the descendants of Abraham's son, Ishmael, became bitter enemies of Israel (see Judges 8:24 and Psalm 83). And they are Israel's bitter enemies to this day. A news article reflects this:

> News photos of Palestinian policemen raising a Nazi-style salute increase anxiety among Holocaust survivors, according to a Bikur Holim Hospital psychiatrist who researched survivors' ability to cope with the present. Dr. Yehudit Rappaports and Dr. Shalom Robinson of the Center for Holocaust Studies found their subjects through Yad Vashem. Those interviewed said anything that reminded them of the Nazi era—including the picture of Nazi-style salutes by Palestinian policemen in Gaza published in the papers—intensified their suffering.[7]
>
> —The Jerusalem Post, January 28, 1995, p.4

Abraham's Other Descendants

Sarah, the beloved wife of Abraham, after bearing the promised child at age 90, finally died at 127. After Abraham sent his servant to seek a wife for his son Isaac, which, incidentally, gives us a wonderful prophetic picture of the Bride of Christ, he obviously felt his calling was completed.

After Isaac married Rebekah, Genesis 25 reports, *"Then again Abraham took a wife, and her name was Keturah. And she bare him Zimran, and Jokshan, and Medan, and Midian, and Ishbak, and Shuah.*

"And Jokshan begat Sheba, and Dedan. And the sons of Dedan were Asshurim, and Letushim, and Leummim. And the

sons of Midian; Ephah, and Epher, and Hanoch, and Abidah, and Eldaah. All these were the children of Keturah.

"And Abraham gave all that he had unto Isaac. But unto the sons of the concubines, which Abraham had, Abraham gave gifts, and sent them away from Isaac his son, while he yet lived, eastward, unto the east country" (Verses 1–6). Abraham, in his old age, raised another family!

Researching the genealogy of this family, we find that the sons of Abraham by Keturah also became bitter enemies of Israel. Therefore, we clearly see again that the Arabs in general who claim Abraham as their father do indeed belong to the same family, and they are related to Israel.

Abraham and 666

Highly interesting is the fact that the death of Abraham is described for us in the 666th verse in the Old Testament. Genesis 25:7–8 reads, *"And these are the days of the years of Abraham's life which he lived, an hundred threescore and fifteen years. Then Abraham gave up the ghost, and died in a good old age, an old man, and full of years; and was gathered to his people."*

When I noticed that the life of the faithful servant Abraham—the father of all who believe—ended at verse 666 in the Old Testament (although fully realizing verses were not numbered in the original manuscripts of the Bible) I found to my great surprise that in the New Testament, it is verse 666 where Jesus, the Son of God, the author and finisher of our faith, describes His own death: *"Behold, we go up to Jerusalem; and the Son of man shall be betrayed unto the chief priests and unto the scribes, and they shall condemn him to death"* (Matthew 20:18).

The distinct difference, however, lies in the fact that contrary to Abraham's death, of which Moses writes, the Lord Jesus utters the prophecy of His *own* death.

Redemption in Prophecy

It was through Abraham and his seed that God would show prophetically how He would redeem mankind from the bondage of sin and the oppression of Satan.

After Abraham finally received the promised offspring, the possibility of him becoming a patriarch of a great nation became real. But then we read the shocking statement addressed to him, *"...Take now thy son, thine only son Isaac, whom thou lovest, and get thee into the land of Moriah; and offer him there for a burnt offering upon one of the mountains which I will tell thee of"* (Genesis 22:2). We must emphasize here the words: *"...thine only son Isaac, whom thou lovest...."* God did not mention the other son, Ishmael, but specifically identified Isaac as the "only son," and heir to the promise. It reminds us of the Lord Jesus Christ, of whom God said, *"...This is my beloved Son, in whom I am well pleased..."* (Matthew 17:5).

Abraham's Most Difficult Time

Abraham was commanded to do the unthinkable: He was to give up his most precious possession, his only beloved son, as God told him to sacrifice Isaac for a burnt offering.

Wouldn't it have been natural at such a crucial time to at least call for a committee meeting of the elders of his household to discuss the matter? Would it not have been appropriate to inform his beloved wife Sarah of this shocking and terrible command God had given him? Perhaps they should have started a prayer meeting to seek a confirmation that it really was God's will. Maybe Abraham misunderstood. After all, he was an old man and he could have been mistaken. Maybe he had a bad dream.

There were many options available to avoid the impossible situation. "Under no circumstances," they must have thought, "should Isaac the beloved son die." After all, he was the answer to their prayers. And he was the *promised* son and only he could fulfill God's pledge that Abraham's seed would become a great nation.

Abraham's Obedience

How did Abraham react? We read in Genesis 22:3, *"And Abraham rose up early in the morning...."* Abraham believed God in spite of the terrifying consequences. There was no question about any mistake. Abraham was a man in tune with God. There was no room for doubt—the fellowship was perfect. God knew what He was saying and Abraham had the absolute certainty of his relationship, which gave him the solid assurance to act in perfect accordance with the Word God spoke! Thus, we have in Abraham a prophetic picture of God's love, *"For God so loved the world, that he gave his only begotten Son, that whosoever believeth in him should not perish, but have everlasting life"* (John 3:16). Abraham was likewise willing to give up his beloved son!

We know how the story ended. Abraham did not have to sacrifice Isaac, but God provided a *substitute.* Genesis 22:13 reads, *"And Abraham lifted up his eyes, and looked, and behold behind him a ram caught in a thicket by his horns: and Abraham went and took the ram, and offered him up for a burnt offering in the stead of his son."*

Abraham's Errors

Although Abraham was faithful, believed in God and acted in accordance with his belief, he also made mistakes as we have seen with the case of Ishmael. Abraham was human, just as you and I are. He was living in a real world. He had to make decisions, care for his family, plan for the future, and manage his little empire.

Parallel to his faithfulness and obedience, he had to think for himself. Going back now in time to verse 4 of Genesis 12, we read, *"So Abram departed, as the LORD had spoken unto him; and Lot went with him: and Abram was seventy and five years old when he departed out of Haran."* This 75-year-old man received a tremendous promise from God, but apparently as *security*, he took Lot along. We read, *"...Lot went with him...."*

It doesn't say whether Abraham urged him to go or whether Lot came voluntarily. It is reasonable to assume that this was one way to assure that the younger Lot would bring forth descendants which could fulfill the promise that from Abraham's family, a great nation would come forth.

But, didn't God clearly instruct him to separate himself from his relatives, parents and siblings? Abraham did everything right, except for "tag–along Lot."

Lot Chose the Left

This little family attachment did not last long, however. The Bible reports, *"And there was a strife between the herdmen of Abram's cattle and the herdmen of Lot's cattle: and the Canaanite and the Perizzite dwelled then in the land"* (Genesis 13:7). Again, we see Abraham dealing wisely and generously. Let's read the story, *"And Abram said unto Lot, Let there be no strife, I pray thee, between me and thee, and between my herdmen and thy herdmen; for we be brethren.*

"Is not the whole land before thee? separate thyself, I pray thee, from me: if thou wilt take the left hand, then I will go to the right; or if thou depart to the right hand, then I will go to the left.

"And Lot lifted up his eyes, and beheld all the plain of Jordan, that it was well watered every where, before the LORD destroyed Sodom and Gomorrah, even as the garden of the LORD, like the land of Egypt, as thou comest unto Zoar. Then Lot chose him all the plain of Jordan; and Lot journeyed east: and they separated themselves the one from the other (Genesis 13:8–11).

Lot didn't prosper, because he didn't act in faith, but on sight: *"And Lot lifted up his eyes...."* He chose based on what he saw. No faith was involved. It would have been natural for him to respond, "You pick first, Uncle Abraham." That was not the case. Lot selfishly looked for his own, and ended up in a most horrible place: Sodom and Gomorrah.

His legacy ended in shame as clearly reported in Genesis 19:36–38, *"Thus were both the daughters of Lot with child by their father. And the firstborn bare a son, and called his name Moab: the same is the father of the Moabites unto this day.*

"And the younger, she also bare a son, and called his name Benammi: the same is the father of the children of Ammon unto this day." The Moabites and the Ammonites also became bitter enemies of Israel later.

Thus we see another beginning of a family conflict in the Middle East. This "family feud" continues to this day, sometimes with weapons of war, sometimes with words.

The following two news articles reflect the conflict that has gone on for so long but now, through negotiation, is coming to an end.

Dear Citizens of Israel. We are adding today another rung in the rising ladder towards the realization of the dream of peace. Full peace with Jordan is attainable. We shall work with Jordan to bring it to fruition.

We all embrace today the Washington Declaration. Israelis, Jordanians, all the lovers of peace and freedom in the world. Tomorrow morning we shall all awaken to a new page in our history. And on this we can say: "This is the day which the LORD hath made; we will rejoice and be glad in it" (Psalm 118:24).

Good evening to you there at home, in Israel. Tomorrow, I hope everything can be different. Peaceful greetings to you from the peace-making. [*Prime Minister Rabin speaking from*

Washington on the eve of the Israeli/Jordanian agreement, July 24, 1994.][8]

—Outpost, April 1994, p.5

Instead of visions of blood and tears there will rise visions of happiness and beauty, life and peace. We are at a historic cross-road. Do we choose the path of the tongues of fire, billowing smoke and rivers of blood, or of blooming deserts, restored wastelands, progress, growth, justice and freedom?

The world has tipped in the direction of economics rather than military might. Armies conquer physical entities, but they cannot conquer qualitative ones. At this stage of the game, objects that may be subject to a military takeover are no longer of value. [*Israeli Foreign Minister Shimon Peres*][9]

—Outpost, April 1994, p.5

The now famous "peace process" will end in a peace for the Jews, Arabs and Christians in the Middle East, and finally for the entire world. However, we must emphasize, this peace will not be a lasting one. It is only temporary because the cause for the division among these people has not been removed. Sin is the cause and sin has never been dealt with in any political process.

Only when Jesus returns and makes an end of the powers of darkness, destroying the wicked with His appearance, will He impute peace that will be everlasting. Only He paid the price for lasting peace. He removed the cause of conflicts, which is sin.

Lot's Descendants Oppose Israel

It is also important to note that approximately 1500 years after Abraham, the prophet Ezekiel reported that the Moabites and Ammonites openly expressed their pleasure in Israel's misfortune, which displeased the Lord greatly.

The statements that the Ammonites and Moabites uttered regarding Judah and Israel were true. Israel indeed had sinned greatly. The House of the Lord was profaned, the land had become desolate, and Israel and Judah were led into captivity. But the Ammonites and Moabites made the mistake of comparing God's chosen people to others. Ezekiel 25:8 reads, *"Thus saith the Lord GOD; Because that Moab and Seir do say, Behold, the house of Judah is like unto all the heathen."*

To get better insight, let's read additional verses to fully understand God's displeasure with the Ammonites and Moabites, *"The word of the LORD came again unto me, saying, Son of man, set thy face against the Ammonites, and prophesy against them; And say unto the Ammonites, Hear the word of the Lord GOD; Thus saith the Lord GOD; Because thou saidst, Aha, against my sanctuary, when it was profaned; and against the land of Israel, when it was desolate; and against the house of Judah, when they went into captivity."*

"...For thus saith the Lord GOD; Because thou hast clapped thine hands, and stamped with the feet, and rejoiced in heart with all thy despite against the land of Israel" (Ezekiel 25:1–3,6).

Here is God's answer which clearly shows that no one, not even relatives, have the right to judge Israel, *"Therefore, behold, I will open the side of Moab from the cities, from his cities which are on his frontiers, the glory of the country, Bethjeshimoth, Baalmeon, and Kiriathaim, Unto the men of the east with the Ammonites, and will give them in possession, that the Ammonites may not be remembered among the nations.*

"And I will execute judgments upon Moab; and they shall know that I am the LORD" (Verses 9–11).

The Apple Of His Eye
We often hear statements, even from Christians, that the Jews crucified Jesus, they rejected the Messiah, and for all their sins

they were cast out into all the nations of the world and became a reproach. Some even go so far as to say that Hitler was right in persecuting the Jews so they would go back to Palestine and fulfill Bible prophecy when they reestablished the nation on Israeli soil!

To make such statements, or even think in such a way, is extremely dangerous, as we have just seen from Ezekiel 25. Actually, the Lord is very sensitive regarding His people of Israel. In Zechariah 2:8 we read, *"For thus saith the LORD of hosts; After the glory hath he sent me unto the nations which spoiled you: for he that toucheth you toucheth the apple of his eye."* Everyone knows how *sensitive* the eye is. A very tiny, almost invisible speck of dust can irritate the eye. And here, we see that God says, *"...for he that toucheth you toucheth the apple of his eye."*

Of course, Israel had sinned greatly. They had cried *"...Crucify him!"* They shouted, *"...We have no king but Caesar!"* And God threatened severe punishment upon the Jewish people. But woe unto those who became the *tools* of the punishment. Jesus said, *"...It is impossible but that offences will come: but woe unto him, through whom they come!"* (Luke 17:1).

God's "Sore Displeasure"

You can sense how God is outraged by the behavior of the heathens when He emphasizes the importance of His love for Zion, *"So the angel that communed with me said unto me, Cry thou, saying, Thus saith the LORD of hosts; I am jealous for Jerusalem and for Zion with a great jealousy"* (Zechariah 1:14). He fails not to give us the reason for His jealously and His displeasure with the heathens, *"And I am very sore displeased with the heathen that are at ease: for I was but a little displeased, and they helped forward the affliction"* (Zechariah 1:15).

Let me give you an example. Assume you are my next door neighbor. Your children are terribly undisciplined. Their behavior becomes so offensive to me that I walk over to your house, take hold of one of the little ones and start spanking. You would certainly be offended, and rightly so, because your children are your responsibility and not mine. They may have deserved punishment because of their bad behavior, but it certainly is not my task to punish them.

This same idea, as it relates to Israel, is expressed precisely in the Word of God.

Indeed, the Jews had sinned terribly. Each violation against God's Holy Covenant is enumerated throughout the Bible and God clearly and unmistakably, through the mouths of the prophets, proclaims the punishment. Yet He says, *"...I was but a little displeased* [with Israel] *and they* [the nations] *helped forward the affliction"* (Zechariah 1:15). Israel's sin did not void God's choosing.

We could fill page after page listing the terrible sins, rebellion, disobedience, and outright blasphemy Israel committed against the Living God, against the Savior who led them out of slavery from Egypt.

He spared judgment upon Israel through the blood of a lamb which the Israelites applied to the door posts and lintel, thus the angel of death passed over them. How mightily He led them through the Red Sea as if on dry ground!

The Egyptian army pursuing them perished in the waters. And yet, deliberately, stubbornly, they refused to heed the Word of God.

Nevertheless, and this is something we need to understand and emphasize strongly, this was and is an internal *family* conflict! It was between God and His own people. While God reveals in detail the sins of Israel and threatens them with consumption by the wrath of His judgment, we see a totally different picture when viewed from the outside.

Two Views Of Israel
Let us see Israel from God's point of view. Notice this is an internal matter, *"And the LORD said unto Moses, How long will this people provoke me? and how long will it be ere they believe me, for all the signs which I have shewed among them? ...Because all those men which have seen my glory, and my miracles, which I did in Egypt and in the wilderness, and have tempted me now these ten times, and have not hearkened to my voice"* (Numbers 14:11;22).

Now let us observe Israel from the *outside*, from the gentile point of view. When we read Numbers 23, for example, it appears that the prophet Balaam is talking about some other nation, not the rebellious nation of Israel. Read his words, *"He hath not beheld iniquity in Jacob, neither hath he seen perverseness in Israel: the LORD his God is with him, and the shout of a king is among them. God brought them out of Egypt; he hath as it were the strength of an unicorn.*

"Surely there is no enchantment against Jacob, neither is there any divination against Israel: according to this time it shall be said of Jacob and of Israel, What hath God wrought! Behold, the people shall rise up as a great lion, and lift up himself as a young lion: he shall not lie down until he eat of the prey, and drink the blood of the slain" (Numbers 23:21–24).

This surely does not seem to fit the description of a rebellious Israel, judging from the reading of previous verses. But it *is* Israel, and we must learn to understand the high calling of these people. Only then are we able to grasp the progression of the prophetic Word in relation to the endtime events and come to the position of understanding God's intention.

Two Views of Your Family
Your family may appear to be wonderfully harmonized to other people. You keep up your property, go to work, pay your bills and taxes, send your children to school, dress them properly,

and attend church regularly. But no one knows what is really happening within the four walls of your home. There may be strife, jealousy, bitterness, and fighting to the extent that your family is on the brink of a disaster. But it is your house, and it is your family. You are exclusively responsible for your family and no one else. You may ask someone to give you advice, to counsel you, to help you, but no one has the right to come to your home and tell you what to do.

Quite often, tribulation in a family will not last indefinitely, especially when one or both walk in the footsteps of the Lord. You make a decision and say, "Lord, I love you with all my heart. I want to do your will in spite of the fact that I am failing almost on a daily basis and I no longer have power within my own house, and my heart aches over the many miseries I have created within our family. But Lord, I totally trust that you will restore my family." The Lord knows, He forgives, and He heals because you thrust yourself into His loving arms!

Walking Wisely Amidst Difficulty
Dear friend, please remember: If you walk wisely in the midst of all your difficulties and your troubles, and don't forget that you are a child of God, then the world can only see that which Balaam saw of the people of Israel. You are then walking in the victory of the Lord Jesus Christ. You are a light to the world and salt to the Earth, regardless of the terrible internal conditions you may find yourself in.

These examples should clearly show that Israel is God's business. He has chosen Israel. It is His family, His responsibility, and He will bring to pass all the promises that were ever uttered to the people of Israel!

The Arabs Today
The Arab nations had been disregarded for many centuries, and suffered greatly under occupation of the British, French and

other European nations. These people were considered to be
nomads of little value to progressive Europe, but their significance became quite suddenly apparent when Israel arose.

The ascent of modern Arab power was made painfully visible to the industrialized world in 1973 when, under the leadership of Egypt, the Arab oil-producing nations quadrupled the
price of oil unexpectedly in response to Israel's victory over
Egypt and Syria in the Yom Kippur War.

The world suffered economic spasms because of that decision. But, regardless from which point of view we observe
these Arab people, the blessing of God through Abraham is
undeniable.

These other sons of Abraham were elevated to previously
unthinkable importance in the eyes of the world. It was the
blessing of the oil from below!

Oil became so significant that in 1991, the U.S.A. under the
jurisdiction of the United Nations, gathered the whole world
against Iraq, which had invaded Kuwait. The short, one-sided
war quickly extinguished the threats of Saddam Hussein's hap-
less army.

Arabs Desire Israel's Jerusalem

The Arabs, most of whom claim to be children of Abraham,
are important players in the endtime. In the days to come we
will see more of that development, as this news headline and
story from *The Jerusalem Post* exhibits:

JERUSALEM: THE STUMBLING STONE

The Foreign Ministry has begun preliminary canvassing of all
foreign embassies to see how many of them would like to
move to Jerusalem once final status negotiations with the
Palestinians are worked out, a Foreign Ministry official said.
"It should be clear that we are not insisting the embassies commit themselves now, but we have to begin planning for zoning

purposes, and that is why we are taking this step. Municipal
Boards must pass everything. We are already behind."[10]

—The Jerusalem Post, 1/28/95, p.3

The foreign ministry desire to move all national embassies to
"western Jerusalem" clearly indicates the government's intention to *surrender* parts of Jerusalem to the Arabs. It also
becomes obvious that the nations of the world desire Israel to
relinquish parts of Jerusalem and do the bidding of the pope
who suggested, in 1967, that Jerusalem be "internationalized."

The Jerusalem conflict is only seen in the beginning now
and many Israeli politicians try desperately to ignore the coming threat. But from the clear statements made by Palestinians,
we see their intention.

JERUSALEM: PLO CAPITAL

Our first goal is the liberation of all occupied territories and
return of all refugees, self-determination for the Palestinians
and the establishment of a Palestinian state whose capital is
Jerusalem. (Yasser Arafat to 19 Arab foreign ministers)[11]

—Dispatch From Jerusalem, December, 1993, p.8

Yasser Arafat and Arab Palestinians consider all of Israel to
be "occupied territory." Their aim is to establish Jerusalem as
the capital of a Palestinian state. While such a goal is pegged
too high at this point, we have to realize that part of Arafat's
desire will be fulfilled. The "Gaza-Jerico First" move has
already been implemented, and more territory is to be given
away to Arab Palestinians in the future.

This is the beginning of the fulfillment or prophecy as
described in Zechariah 12:2–3, *"Behold, I will make
Jerusalem a cup of trembling unto all the people round about,
when they shall be in the siege both against Judah and against
Jerusalem.*

"And in that day will I make Jerusalem a burdensome stone for all people: all that burden themselves with it shall be cut in pieces, though all the people of the earth be gathered together against it."

Final Unity

The family conflict in the Middle East cannot be solved by diplomats, not by the United States, or Europe, and not by the United Nations. Nor are the Arabs capable of bringing forth peace that will last.

It is the Lord Himself, the Prince of Peace, who will accomplish it because He has paid the price for peace. He alone is able to bring forth reconciliation; not composed by clever politicians on a piece of paper, but He will command peace based on His words, *"...It is finished!"* These words are sealed in His own eternally valid blood. The real price for real peace is paid in full!

When Israel finally sees Him whom they have pierced, and recognize Him, the Savior of the world, the Messiah of Israel, it will not be kept hidden, but will also touch the surrounding nations. Then God will bring to pass all the promises He has given to all of Abraham's children.

The prophet Isaiah predicted this unifying power of the Lord over 2,700 years ago, *"In that day shall there be a highway out of Egypt to Assyria, and the Assyrian shall come into Egypt, and the Egyptian into Assyria, and the Egyptians shall serve with the Assyrians.*

"In that day shall Israel be the third with Egypt and with Assyria, even a blessing in the midst of the land.

"Whom the LORD of hosts shall bless, saying, Blessed be Egypt my people, and Assyria the work of my hands, and Israel mine inheritance" (Isaiah 19:23–25).

In a parallel fashion, it is therefore of immense importance that we as believers in the Lord Jesus Christ never permit ourselves to be deceived by the self-exalted idea that we can engineer political peace before Jesus returns. Never will we be able to establish a nation or world of peace and institute Christian government in the land. It simply will not happen, because we do not have the promise of the Scripture to support such ideas.

CHAPTER 5

Israel:
The Greatest
Endtime Sign

Summary

In spite of shocking and startling developments experienced during this century, the greatest of all end-time signs—and yet the least empha-sized—is the return of the Jewish people to the Promised Land and the founding of the State of Israel.

The Testimony of Charles Spurgeon, 1910

Although we have spoken of Israel several times in previous chapters, it is necessary for us to take a closer look at the re-establishment of this nation, in the light of prophecy.

Only few and far between are the servants of God who follow the Lord with all of their hearts, and therefore are able also to recognize the future.

One such person was Charles Spurgeon. Back in 1910, before Israel became a nation, and when there appeared to be no possibility of the Jews coming back to the Holy Land, he taught that Israel would be a nation, just as Ezekiel 36 and 37 stated:

> The meaning of our text, as opened up by the context, is most evidently, if words mean anything, first, that there shall be a political restoration of the Jews to their own land and to their own nationality; and then, secondly, there is in the text, and in the context, a most plain declaration, that there shall be a spiritual restoration, a conversion in fact, of the tribes of Israel.
>
> They are to have a national prosperity which shall make them famous; nay, so glorious shall they be that Egypt, and Tyre, and Greece, and Rome, shall all forget their glory in the greater splendor of the throne of David. If there be meaning in words this must be the meaning of this chapter.
>
> I wish never to learn the art of tearing God's meaning out of His own words. If there be anything clear and plain, the literal sense and meaning of this passage—a meaning not to be spirited or spiritualized away—must be evident that both the two and the ten tribes of Israel are to be restored to their own land, and that a king is to rule over them.

Israel's Desire For Peace

Let us analyze the progressive development that is taking place today, which will lead Israel into union with the new world order dominated by Europe. Today we see Israel mingling with her former enemies, not because they have adopted a new philosophy that makes them love each other, but because of the notion of a negotiated peace.

Israel is overwhelmed with the prospect of actually living in peace with her Arab neighbors. She thinks peace will come. But the Bible says: *"For when they shall say, Peace and safety; then sudden destruction cometh upon them, as travail upon a woman with child; and they shall not escape"* (1st Thessalonians 5:3).

Israel: The Object of Prophecy
We also do well to understand that the endtime signs given by the Lord are *specifically directed to Israel.* When Jesus explained the endtime events to His disciples, with the accompanying signs that are to take place before His coming, He addressed them to the people of Israel.

We have two very plain characteristics mentioned in Matthew 24 which identify a certain people. *"Then let them which be in Judaea flee into the mountains"* (verse 16). This is a *geographical* reference, not meant for the Church of Jesus Christ. If we reside in the U.S.A., Canada, Europe, or other parts of the world, we cannot flee to the mountains of Judea because they are located in Israel.

Further, Jesus is identifying a prayer object, *"But pray ye that your flight be not in the winter, neither on the sabbath day"* (verse 20).

The Sabbath is given only to the Jews. We read in the Holy Scripture regarding the Sabbath: *"Speak thou also unto the children of Israel, saying, Verily my sabbaths ye shall keep: for it is a sign between me and you throughout your generations; that ye may know that I am the LORD that doth sanctify you"* (Exodus 31:13). Therefore, the great sign of the endtimes for the gentiles and the church is Israel!

Israel's Ancient Sin

What is Israel's aim for the future? She is now facing her original national sin. Almost 3,500 years ago, the people of Israel
were in the Promised Land. God had fulfilled everything that
He had promised concerning their entry, but Israel refused to
be chosen by God, to be a uniquely different nation, to do His
bidding.

God identified the deepest reason for this, stating plainly
that the people of Israel did not want God to rule over them.
They rejected outright the words of God as given through
Moses: *"For thou art an holy people unto the LORD thy God,
and the LORD hath chosen thee to be a peculiar people unto
himself, above all the nations that are upon the earth"*
(Deuteronomy 14:2).

What a tremendous promise this was! Israel was to be
"...above all the nations that are upon the earth." We know
from history that many nations have tried to become above all
other nations.

This is quite evident in America, too. We consider ourselves
to be a special nation. Most of us would claim that the U.S.A.
is the greatest nation in the history of the world. Many other
nations before us committed this same sin, but, the dust of their
ruins bears witness against them.

The Holy Nation of Christians

Who are we as Christians, then? First Peter 2:9 answers, *"But
ye are a chosen generation, a royal priesthood, an holy nation,
a peculiar people; that ye should shew forth the praises of him
who hath called you out of darkness into his marvellous light."*
We, the Church of Jesus Christ, are also a peculiar people. We
are a chosen generation. We are a holy nation. But this holy
nation is not to be found in any political identity such as
America, Canada, France, England, China, or any other place
in the world. This holy nation resides within the nations of the

world and each individual member of this holy nation is known by the Lord Himself.

We have all the reasons to believe that this holy nation is about to be completed, and when that happens, when the last one of the gentiles is added, we will be *raptured* to our Lord, in His presence for all eternity!

Israel's Request For A King

The rebellious statement Israel made against the living God by requesting a king in order to be "just like the other nations" did not simply fizzle out. Instead, it climaxed some 1,000 years later. We read in John 19:15, *"...We have no king but Caesar!"* The full weight of their forefather's statement, reflecting the desire to be part of the family of nations, to be just like any other people, comes to fruition, *"...We have no king but Caesar!"* Israel will yet be confronted with this statement when the nations of the Earth shall gather to battle against Jerusalem!

Israel's Steps Toward Peace

At this moment, everything looks like the Holy Land is headed toward a negotiated "peace." Increasing numbers of former enemy nations of Israel are establishing diplomatic relationships. The possibility of increased commerce across national borders is very tempting, and no doubt Israel's economy will continue to grow strongly.

But all of these positive signs will never change the prophetic Word. Jesus says, *"I am come in my Father's name, and ye receive me not: if another shall come in his own name, him ye will receive"* (John 5:43). Israel is on her way to be part of the last gentile world empire and she will accept the Antichrist.

Only when we understand these events from a spiritual aspect, can we begin to comprehend what is happening in the political, economic, and religious world. With this in mind, we should better understand the political events that are taking place in the world today. If we don't know the end result, we may well be swallowed up by the enthusiasm of the false peace that is being developed today.

Antichrist: The Master Deceiver

When the Word of God identifies the work of the Antichrist, we read the following in 2nd Thessalonians 2:7–11, *"For the mystery of iniquity doth already work: only he who now letteth will let, until he be taken out of the way. And then shall that Wicked be revealed, whom the Lord shall consume with the spirit of his mouth, and shall destroy with the brightness of his coming:*

"Even him, whose coming is after the working of Satan with all power and signs and lying wonders, And with all deceivableness of unrighteousness in them that perish; because they received not the love of the truth, that they might be saved.

"And for this cause God shall send them strong delusion, that they should believe a lie."

This Scripture makes two things clear: One, the work of the Antichrist is successful through deception, and two, rejection of God's offer of love (John 3:16) is the cause for believing a lie.

CHAPTER 6

The Mystery of Iniquity and the Rapture

Summary

When the Apostle Paul prophesied about the rising of the Antichrist and the last world empire, he used the term "the mystery of iniquity" to describe a certain person whose power would have a devastating result for the entire world. The reason for calling it "the mystery of iniquity" shows that something is hidden, and is not generally recognized. The final revelation will only occur when the *hindering element* is removed. In the meantime, we already see the beginning of *the mystery of iniquity* today.

Who, or What is "the Mystery of Iniquity"?
The subject title of this chapter is found in 2nd Thessalonians 2:7, *"For the mystery of iniquity doth already work: only he who now letteth will let, until he be taken out of the way."*

The Apostle Paul makes it very plain that this "mystery of iniquity" was already at work during his time, almost 2,000 years ago. Let us look at the context in which the "mystery of iniquity" appears. *"Let no man deceive you by any means: for that day shall not come, except there come a falling away first, and that man of sin be revealed, the son of perdition; Who opposeth and exalteth himself above all that is called God, or that is worshipped; so that he as God sitteth in the temple of God, shewing himself that he is God.*

"Remember ye not, that, when I was yet with you, I told you these things? And now ye know what withholdeth that he might be revealed in his time.

"For the mystery of iniquity doth already work: only he who now letteth will let, until he be taken out of the way. And then shall that Wicked be revealed, whom the Lord shall consume with the spirit of his mouth, and shall destroy with the brightness of his coming:

"Even him, whose coming is after the working of Satan with all power and signs and lying wonders, And with all deceivableness of unrighteousness in them that perish; because they received not the love of the truth, that they might be saved.

"And for this cause God shall send them strong delusion, that they should believe a lie: That they all might be damned who believed not the truth, but had pleasure in unrighteousness" (2nd Thessalonians 2:3–12).

Here in these few verses, we see clearly that "the mystery of iniquity," the spirit of Antichrist, was at work already at the beginning of the church. Why? Because he is the product of Satan, the great opponent of God, *"...Who opposeth and exalteth himself above all that is called God...."*

Also revealed here is the removal of the church, *"...until he* [the church] *be taken out of the way."*

Then the identification of the Antichrist, *"...that wicked..."* will take place and thereby his defeat becomes apparent, not through some confrontational battle, but simply *"...with the brightness of his* [Jesus'] *coming."*

The Great Delusion

If I were to choose another key word in these few verses, it would be "delusion." Although the church is still on Earth, the work of the spirit of the Antichrist is in full swing. The man of sin who receives power from Satan produces *"...signs and lying wonders..."* for the express purpose of deceiving those who *"...received not the love of the truth...."*

How this deception is a reality in our day, was amplified by an article in *U.S.News and World Report* (December 20th, 1993). When a copy of a magazine came to my desk with the lead story on the front page titled "WHO WAS JESUS? A NEW LOOK AT HIS WORDS AND DEEDS," my thoughts immediately went to 1st Corinthians chapter 1, verses 18 through 25, *"For the preaching of the cross is to them that perish foolishness; but unto us which are saved it is the power of God. For it is written, I will destroy the wisdom of the wise, and will bring to nothing the understanding of the prudent.*

"Where is the wise? where is the scribe? where is the disputer of this world? hath not God made foolish the wisdom of this world? For after that in the wisdom of God the world by wisdom knew not God, it pleased God by the foolishness of preaching to save them that believe.

"For the Jews require a sign, and the Greeks seek after wisdom: But we preach Christ crucified, unto the Jews a stumblingblock, and unto the Greeks foolishness;

"But unto them which are called, both Jews and Greeks, Christ the power of God, and the wisdom of God. Because the

foolishness of God is wiser than men; and the weakness of God is stronger than men."

As I read the *U.S.News* article, I saw how clearly it demonstrated that men's wisdom is foolishness, from statements like this:

> He is depicted as an eloquent preacher and skilled healer, an exorcist and miracle worker. Now scholars are unearthing the historical truth of his life and times. Jesus proclaimed that the kingdom of God had arrived, but his view of the kingdom defied conventional wisdom.
>
> Whether or not the miracle accounts are more symbolic stories than biography, it appears to most scholars that Jesus probably did perform some miracles. "We may not be able to ascertain which miracles are authentic," says Professor Tambasco of Georgetown University. "We do have a sense that all of the stories are reworked. We can, however, be reasonably sure that all of the healings taken together witness to the fact of the miracles in the life of Jesus."[12]

What this professor is doing with such statements is sowing additional seeds of doubt and confusion, thus typifying the *"...great falling away..."* because they *"...received not the love of the truth."*

Waiting For the Rapture, Not the Day of Christ
We do well to emphasize that the early Christians, during Paul's time, were waiting for the coming of the Lord. There was, however, seemingly a misunderstanding regarding 1) the coming of the Lord and 2) the gathering unto Him.

Obviously someone was preaching, writing letters, and circulating rumors that *"...the day of Christ is at hand"* (2nd Thessalonians 2:2). As a result, these believers were greatly troubled. In 1st Thessalonians 4:16–18, the apostle wrote to them about the Rapture. Now, however, someone was teaching that *"...the day of Christ is at hand."* Paul explained that the communications, which had confused them, had not come from him. His great concern was expressed clearly in these two verses, *"Now we beseech you, brethren, by the coming of our Lord Jesus Christ, and by our gathering together unto him That ye be not soon shaken in mind, or be troubled, neither by spirit, nor by word, nor by letter as from us, as that the day of Christ is at hand"* (2nd Thessalonians 2:1–2).

Paul then went on to describe the successive events which are to take place. First, the hindering element, which is the Church of Jesus Christ, must be taken out of the way. Only the departure of the church with the Holy Spirit will permit the revelation of the Antichrist.

The Removal of the Comforter

Someone may now object and say, "How can people be saved if the Holy Spirit departs?" That is a legitimate question.

Let's clarify the answer with a counter-question, "When did the Holy Spirit come?" The Lord Jesus states in John 14:16–18, *"And I will pray the Father, and he shall give you another Comforter, that he may abide with you for ever; Even the Spirit of truth; whom the world cannot receive, because it seeth him not, neither knoweth him: but ye know him; for he dwelleth with you, and shall be in you.*

"I will not leave you comfortless: I will come to you." This Scripture identifies the office of the Holy Spirit as being the "Comforter." That means when the Holy Spirit as the Comforter has departed with the church, then there will be no more comfort. Those who will believe in Jesus Christ after the Rapture, during the Great Tribulation, will not be comforted with the hope of the Rapture.

This seems natural because the masses of people remaining after the Rapture will refuse to give their lives over to Jesus.

Rather, they will continue to live "in the flesh" in the world. But during the Great Tribulation they will have to forfeit their lives for Jesus, if they decide to convert to Him.

Please note that in John 14:18, the Lord specifically says, *"I will not leave you comfortless: I will come to you."* This confirms the perfect unity which we call the Trinity, an established doctrine in the Holy Scripture. Jesus has gone away, but He is coming again through the Holy Spirit. Thus, He can say, *"...I will come to you."* The full revelation of the knowledge of the mystery of the Trinity will then be revealed. *"At that day ye shall know that I am in my Father, and ye in me, and I in you"* (verse 20).

The Day of Christ
After the church, with the Comforter, the Holy Spirit, is taken out of the way, we read in 2nd Thessalonians 2:8, *"...then shall that wicked be revealed...."*

Finally, the ultimate confrontation between light and darkness will take place. The end result is "the day of Christ," when He appears in great power and glory for the purpose of making an end of the Antichrist, *"...whom the Lord shall consume with the spirit of his mouth, and shall destroy with the brightness of his coming"* (verse 8).

Comfortless Gospel
Therefore, the false gospel being propagated today by modern theology, which denies the coming of Jesus at any moment, is, in reality, a comfortless gospel!

The Scotsman magazine published the following on May 28th, 1994, written by Frank Pilkington, showing the extent of confusion:

> Being brought up in the Catholic religion since I was born, you can imagine how difficult it was for me to understand and

accept my gift of being psychic. Christian people were always led to believe that God was above us and that the Devil was somewhere on the outside just waiting to tempt us to do wrong. It is my belief that both entities can be contained and that by the discovery of ourselves and the understanding of our motives, we can make clear choices as to what is good and what is evil. In doing so, we can determine our own spiritual path.

New age thinking will allow our spirituality to grow much more as we leave behind the effects of Saturn, the planet that rules the churches. All religions are in for a big shakeup over the next two years, as Saturn has now entered Pisces, and I think that the religious hierarchy will need to learn how to merge and transcend, because if they don't allow a margin for alternatives their laws will become too rigid.[13]

One thing is now certain: The "next two years" have passed and no "major shakeup" of all religion has occurred. Unfortunately, such confusion is being taken seriously and many are caught in such astrological deceptions.

The Strong Delusion
The Scripture does not fail to inform us of the exact tools and avenues Satan uses to bring about his visible kingdom on Earth. It is striking to see that the Devil's amazing master plan for deception is not only allowed by God, but even sealed by Him with the words, *"And for this cause God shall send them strong delusion, that they should believe a lie"* (2nd Thessalonians 2:11).

To summarize, the true Gospel is being preached to call people to Christ and prepare for *"...our gathering together unto him."* But in parallel, the day of Christ is being prepared by God's allowance of Satan's master plan of deception, *"That they all might be damned who believed not the truth, but had pleasure in unrighteousness"* (verse 12). The climax of this progressive deception is accomplished by the religious aspect, which is "the mystery of iniquity."

To summarize, the "day of Christ" (not the Rapture, but His literal return to the Mount of Olives) cannot take place because the Antichrist is not revealed. But the revelation of the Antichrist cannot materialize because the church has not been removed. It is impossible for the epitome of darkness to be revealed parallel to the existence of the church on Earth because the church, wherein dwells God the Holy Spirit, is still present on Earth!

Later in this book, I will discuss, in greater detail, the events that lead to the final deception.

CHAPTER 7

Mystery Babylon and Her Power

Summary

Who, or what is Mystery Babylon? This chapter answers much-debated questions. Investigating the covenant of seven years reveals the success of the Antichrist and the creation of the image of the beast, which is technologically possible today. Mystery Babylon's intoxicating political, religious, and economic fornication are dealt with in this chapter.

Mystery Babylon and Her Power

The term "Mystery Babylon" appears only one time in the Bible, in Revelation 17:5, *"And upon her forehead was a name written, MYSTERY, BABYLON THE GREAT, THE MOTHER OF HARLOTS AND ABOMINATIONS OF THE EARTH."* This is the climax of abomination, the most horrifying title anyone could possibly be named with. We know that this is the epitome of evil during the endtime as set forth in the book of Revelation. It is the time which the prophets spoke of many centuries ago.

The Day of the Lord

To fully understand this terrible time, let us hear what the prophets of the Old Testament had to say.

Zephaniah uttered these words, *"The great day of the LORD is near, it is near, and hasteth greatly, even the voice of the day of the LORD: the mighty man shall cry there bitterly. That day is a day of wrath, a day of trouble and distress, a day of wasteness and desolation, a day of darkness and gloominess, a day of clouds and thick darkness"* (Zephaniah 1:14–15). What day is he speaking of? It is the day of the Lord when He comes back in great power and glory to finalize the defeat of the Antichrist and the entire new world order system.

The prophet Joel described this most horrible time with these words, *"The earth shall quake before them; the heavens shall tremble: the sun and the moon shall be dark, and the stars shall withdraw their shining: And the LORD shall utter his voice before his army: for his camp is very great: for he is strong that executeth his word: for the day of the LORD is great and very terrible; and who can abide it?"* (Joel 2:10–11).

Jeremiah specifically emphasized that this is a unique day, never to be repeated, *"Alas! for that day is great, so that none is like it: it is even the time of Jacob's trouble, but he shall be saved out of it"* (Jeremiah 30:7).

Later in history, the Lord Jesus confirmed this prophecy when He said in Matthew 24:21, *"For then shall be great tribulation, such as was not since the beginning of the world to this time, no, nor ever shall be."*

These and many other Scriptures identify the last part of the endtimes as the time of the Tribulation. It will last seven years and result in the greatest bloodbath humanity has ever known.

The Covenant of Seven Years

The Great Tribulation begins with the Antichrist confirming an apparently already-existing covenant. Daniel 9:27 documents it with these words, *"And he shall confirm the covenant with many for one week: and in the midst of the week he shall cause the sacrifice and the oblation to cease, and for the over-spreading of abominations he shall make it desolate, even until the consummation, and that determined shall be poured upon the desolate."*

It is important to emphasize at this point that the seven-year Tribulation must be divided in two equal parts, that is, 3.5 years each. The first 3.5 years will be a time of jubilation. There will be peace, prosperity, and riches so overwhelming that the people of the world will unconditionally support this new world order system led by him who the Bible refers to as the Antichrist.

Antichrist's Success

It is stunning to realize how successful he will be. Revelation 13:3 proclaims, *"...and all the world wondered after the beast."*

This beast is incomparable in human history, thus, the people ask, *"...Who is like unto the beast?..."* (Revelation 13:4). Quite obviously, he is also a military genius, *"...who is able to make war with him?"* (verse 4b).

Ultimately, the ecumenical movement, the World Council of Churches, the United Nations and whoever else may be involved in the work toward unity, will finally have merged into one powerful religion. Thus, the Bible says, *"And all that dwell upon the earth shall worship him..."* (verse 8).

There is an exception, however. Verse 8 continues, *"...whose names are not written in the book of life of the Lamb slain from the foundation of the world."* We see a group of people who will *not* participate to the end in this one world movement. These people are the Jews, God's chosen ones. Although they will be deceived by the Antichrist during the first half of the Tribulation, they will not follow him during the second half. Let me explain.

Jacob's Trouble

We previously quoted Jeremiah 30:7, but for clarity's sake, let's read it again, *"Alas! for that day is great, so that none is like it: it is even the time of Jacob's trouble; but he shall be saved out of it."* Notice here that the time is called "Jacob's trouble."

What is the purpose of this? Why not "Israel's trouble" or "Judah's trouble"? Why "Jacob's trouble"? I believe the reason is found in the fact that the nature of Jacob—his very name means "deceiver" or "supplanter"—was never done away with. Israel until this day incorporates strong aspects of this "Jacob nature."

We find the name Jacob 377 times in the Bible, but Israel is mentioned 2,600 times. However, the "Jacob nature" is incorporated in national Israel. Israel's desire for self-righteousness, to bring about salvation through the law, has never ceased. Thus, Israel's old Jacob nature will go through the judgment period of 3.5 years of deception.

But then, a 3.5 year corrective Tribulation will end in her self-recognition and subsequent salvation.

Satan the Imitator

Again, we must point out that Satan, the Devil, also called the dragon, is not able to create but can only imitate. Thus, in Revelation 13, we see the dragon giving power and authority to the beast that comes *"...out of the sea."* Verse 2b says, *"...and the dragon gave him his power, and his seat, and great authority."* Here we see the counterfeit. The dragon is giving his whole endorsement and places authority and power in the hands of the Antichrist, just as the Father, who is in heaven, has given all things to the Son.

When carefully reading Revelation 13, we recognize four distinct identities who are the main characters in the great worldwide deception.

The Antichrist

"And I stood upon the sand of the sea, and saw a beast rise up out of the sea" (Revelation 13:1). We identify him as the Antichrist. He comes out of the sea of nations. No one really knows who he is and where he originates from. Many scholars are convinced he will have a Jewish background. I agree because from Israel comes the blessing and the curse, salvation and judgment. Men who have been and are responsible for world-changing events are mostly Jewish.

Satan

The great dragon, the old serpent, who also carries the title of the Devil and Satan, is the one who *"...gave him* (Antichrist, the first beast) *his power, and his seat, and great authority."*

Satan and the Antichrist are United

We see both receiving worship, *"And they worshipped the dragon which gave power unto the beast: and they worshipped the beast, saying, Who is like unto the beast? who is able to make war with him?"*

The False Prophet

"And I beheld another beast coming up out of the earth..."
(verse 11). This other beast does not come out of the sea, out
of the unidentifiable masses of people, but *"...up out of the
earth...."* Thus, his location must be geographically identifiable. This second beast already possesses power and authority.
We also recognize his religious governance.

In contrast to the first beast who received everything
directly from the dragon, we see the second beast already in
possession of power, *"And he exerciseth all the power of the
first beast..."* (verse 12).

*"And deceiveth them that dwell on the earth by the means
of those miracles which he had power to do in the sight of the
beast"* (verse 14). And in verse 15: *"And he had power to give
life unto the image of the beast...."* We clearly see that the second beast *supports* the first. The Bible says, *"...he had two
horns like a lamb, and he spake as a dragon"* (verse 11). This
is an amazing statement, *"...like a lamb...."* He is not the
Lamb of God but an *imitation*. He claims to be Christ (or representative) but is not.

The Image

Finally, there is *"...the image of the beast...."* Where does this
image come from? It is not identical with the Antichrist, neither Satan, nor the false prophet but this "image" is actually
manmade.

The false prophet is the initiating power to create such an
image, *"...saying to them that dwell on the earth, that they
should make an image to the beast, which had the wound by a
sword, and did live"* (Revelation 13:14b). Then we read in
verse 15 that the false prophet *"...had power to give life unto
the image of the beast...."* Using a modern-day metaphor, it
would indicate that the false prophet is the one who supplies
the software for this "image of the beast."

The next sentence, however, is startling because it shows that the ultimate authority will then lie in the hands of this manmade image, *"... the image of the beast should both speak, and cause that as many as would not worship the image of the beast should be killed."*

It is this manufactured image which has the authority regarding who should be killed. We need not belabor the point that the technology exists today to produce such a deadly machine.

An article from *Newsweek* should convince you of this:

The marriage of man (or woman) and machine is one of the most intriguing images in science fiction. From the Bionic Woman to RoboCop, these creatures are blessed with bodies that just won't quit and brains (computers) at the top of the evolutionary scale. You ain't seen nothin' yet!

To some futurists, the most alluring possibility is what science fiction calls "wetware," the linking of the human brain and computers. The word "wet" refers to the brain; its play on hardware (computer equipment) and software (computer programs). In this vision, they would be connected directly with machines. The computer could literally read your brain waves, your thoughts—all your thoughts, mundane and majestic.

Virtual telepathy is probably generations away, (if it ever happens), but researchers are currently experimenting with devices that might someday evolve into a kind of wetware. Scientists are trying to create computer images through electrodes attached to the brain, arm or facial muscles. These systems work by translating the electrical signals generated by the nervous system into patterns that computers can read. The research helps increase computer access for disabled people who could substitute a blink of an eye or the twitch of a cheek for fingers on the keyboard. [14]

—Newsweek, May 30, 1994, p.68

Total Control

We must take special interest in "the other beast," the false prophet. He is obviously in agreement with the dragon who gives power unto the first beast, because he supports his platform economically, militarily and religiously. The "other beast," the false prophet, is also the great inventor of a new world religion. His product will implement, for the first time in human history, total control.

On the level of religion, through his "miraculous" creation of the "image of the beast," he will make sure that all people on the face of the Earth will worship the image of the beast or be killed.

The Mark

On the economic-financial level as well, the false prophet institutes a foolproof system, *"And he causeth all, both small and great, rich and poor, free and bond, to receive a mark in their right hand, or in their foreheads: And that no man might buy or sell, save he that had the mark, or the name of the beast, or the number of his name"* (Revelation 13:16–17). That's total control! In order to identify Mystery Babylon, therefore, we must look for a person supported by a system which exercises supreme authority in religion and economy.

Let's look at the way our world is being changed so that such authority will not be so difficult to be established.

There are plans on the drawing board right here in America that seem to be preparing for that day, when all must have the "mark" in order to survive, buy, sell or trade. It may not necessarily be a deliberate preparation, but we can see that it is leading in the general direction of economic control.

An assigned number for every state resident would make for more efficient government, saving tax dollars, according to a proposal by a cabinet level commission. The state could have, in place, a system, that assigns every North Carolinian a computer identification number or code, that could be used to keep track of information about the person by 1997, commission members said. The commission has not ruled out using Social Security numbers. But it is not sure whether Federal law, which contains restrictions over the use of Social Security numbers, will allow it. The proposal could also raise fears that the state is collecting too much information about its residents, commission members said, much like the all-knowing "Big Brother" in George Orwell's novel, *1984*.[15]

—The News and Observer, February 9, 1995

Control Welcomed

In order to better understand what the Scripture has predicted, we must not view all things in the modern world from a negative point of view. Surely every decent upright citizen, working for a living, paying taxes, doing what is right, is in favor of curtailing waste, crime, welfare fraud, and the like. With proper electronic control, the drug trade, for example, could be wiped out.

We must also take into consideration the many billions, if not trillions, of dollars which the IRS is incapable of collecting due to insufficient control. They could be collected, but are not, and subsequently, they must be made up by taxpayers. The more this system of control is developed and refined, the broader the support from the general public will be. With the new efficient collection of taxes, perhaps the rates could even be lowered!

Political Babylon

Mystery Babylon is called a woman, later identified as a city, *"And the woman which thou sawest is that great city, which reigneth over the kings of the earth"* (Revelation 17:18). From this, we learn that Mystery Babylon not only has religious and economic authority, but also political. Otherwise, we would not read that the *"...kings of the earth...,"* the political leaders, have any dealings with her.

The fact that Mystery Babylon commits fornication is also significant. If this woman, which is also identified as a city, has some political dealings with presidents, prime ministers, and kings, it would be quite normal.

But the union here between this woman and the kings of the Earth constitutes fornication, thus, she is not only called a whore, but "the great whore."

The word "fornication" is used 36 times in the Bible, mainly identifying an illicit sexual relationship. Relating to Mystery Babylon, however, "fornication" is mentioned eight times and is emphasized in relationship to prosperity.

For example, *"For all nations have drunk of the wine of the wrath of her fornication, and the kings of the earth have committed fornication with her, and the merchants of the earth are waxed rich through the abundance of her delicacies"* (Revelation 18:3).

Worldwide Fornication
Besides the "kings"—the rulers of this world—the inhabitants of the Earth will commit fornication with her as well. The whole world participates in her fornication through the substance of "the wine." The result thereof is identified in verse 2. They *"...have been made drunk with the wine of her fornication."* This is not some local matter whereby the trespass of fornication is being committed with a king or two, but it says here, *"...the kings of the earth."*

Mystery Babylon, therefore, is so powerful that the rulers of Earth have to deal with her in order to be part of this great successful one world system. And it is by the great whore that the inhabitants of the Earth are made drunk, intoxicated with the religious, political, and economic success.

Worldwide Communication

We all know that effective worldwide communication was impossible only one hundred years ago. The main modes of transportation were ships, horses and buggies, and later the steam engine. There was a definite limit to communication.

To operate a system that includes all the people of the world, it must incorporate the capability to instantly communicate globally. Today, it is possible to communicate around the world instantaneously by satellites, and one can travel to any place by jet, sometimes faster than the speed of sound.

And with the advancement of computer technology, there is often no need to even travel. Teleworking and teleconferencing, conducting business without travelling anywhere, are becoming extremely popular trends. That means a truly worldwide system, which was never possible before now, has become a reality!

Intoxicated Babylon

Let us also note again that the people of the Earth are, in a metaphorical sense, being made drunk. A driver, for example, who knows it is illegal to drive while intoxicated, also knows it is dangerous.

After drinking, He nevertheless takes command of a vehicle because he thinks he is well-able, and actually believes he is in sufficient command of all his abilities. He does not realize the danger he presents to himself and the public. While his mind was free from alcohol, he was able to operate a vehicle safely. But now that he is drunk, judgment and physical ability are severely impaired and the over-confidence results in a possible tragedy for himself and others.

We don't have to be experts to realize that the world is already intoxicated with the "wine" of the "fornication" of "the great whore" to such an extent that they actually believe all problems can be solved by their own initiatives.

Intoxicating Democracy

Is there anyone left who does not believe that democracy, the system whereby people rule themselves, is the best of all political philosophies? Is there any political institution or center of higher learning that realizes we cannot help ourselves or solve the problems of our world outside of God?

Each political system, whether it is democracy, socialism, communism, Nazism, or dictatorship, is fully convinced that it possesses, within itself, the ability to solve all problems. Today, for the first time in history, humanity has apparently decided to be identified with one system: democracy.

Intoxicating Education

Just try to go to a place of higher learning and propose that we should first teach our students to obey God who created heaven and Earth, so that they might begin to understand who they are and what the purpose of their being is. Surely we would be mocked for making such an old-fashioned, out-moded, and superstitious religious statement. This clearly shows mankind at large is already spiritually drunk and does not know who he is, where he is going, and what the future will be.

Just think what a professor at Yale, Harvard, Oxford, MIT, Princeton, or any other top-rated university would say if you were to tell them the plain truth about man's condition: *"But we are all as an unclean thing, and all our righteousnesses are as filthy rags; and we all do fade as a leaf; and our iniquities, like the wind, have taken us away"* (Isaiah 64:6). They would dismiss such a statement as utter nonsense and question your mental state.

Self Love: Babylon

In the religious world too, even in Christianity, it is no longer accepted that man is corrupt, lost, unable to help himself, and on his way to eternal damnation. Only a very small minority would accept the statement, *"...we are all as an unclean thing, and all our righteousnesses are as filthy rags...."* That is contrary to the teaching of the world and "professing" Christianity at large. As a matter of fact, today's society (made drunk with the wine of the whore's "self image") is being taught to super-emphasize the nobility of man, to think positive, and to do everything in its power to build up "self-esteem."

While our prisons are overflowing and lawlessness is rampant, we are told that the reason is not because of sin, but rather it is because of the prisoner's upbringing, his surroundings, or circumstances such as economic deprivation.

Someone may be a vicious murderer, but because his lawyer can convince the judge and jury that the defendant had such a terrible life as a child, he is found "not guilty," or given a reduced sentence.

Murderers and all manner of criminals are filling our prisons and are being taught diligently that if they begin to love themselves and understand that their low self-esteem and self-worth is responsible for their actions, they could reenter society as reformed persons.

Most people today actually believe that sinful and corrupt men can be changed by proper analysis of their "self" and behavior-altering programs. Words such as prisons, inmates, convicts, and the like are no longer used. They are not "politically correct." A criminal in prison becomes a "resident" of a "correctional institution."

Is it necessary to point out that the world is intoxicated by the fornication with Mystery Babylon? Do we need anymore proof? Obviously not!

Christian Babylon

What is most shocking of all, however, is that within Christianity and I must emphasize, within born-again Bible-believing Christian ministries, this intoxication is having an affect as well. The proper way to solve a personality conflict is no longer through Biblical counseling which would lead the sinner to repentance. Sending such a person to a "Christian" psychologist or psychiatrist is today's answer. Woe unto the pastor who tells a person, "Repent of your sins so the Lord, in His grace, may restore you!" Such a pastor or minister could find himself facing resolute opposition and a possible lawsuit.

Our judicial system no longer accepts the spiritual authority of a church leader, and only a so-called "properly trained counselor" with earned degrees in psychology or psychiatry is deemed qualified to analyze a person with a problem and prescribe the proper remedy.

Jesus Renews, Psychology Repairs
I must point out that psychology, psychiatry, or other types of unbiblical counselling, nevertheless, do help. We cannot deny the success of many Christian psychologists who are helping hundreds of thousands of people to deal with their problems. After all, a good talk with a well-trained psychologist may do wonders. But at the same time, a good talk with anyone else could do wonders as well.

People who belong to the Buddhist, Hindu, or Islamic religions go to their counselors and receive help too. The truth, however, is that when you come to Jesus and wholeheartedly confess your sins to Him and repent of them, you will not just be helped, you will be totally liberated! The psychologist may help, but Jesus renews! The Bible says, *"If the Son therefore shall make you free, ye shall be free indeed"* (John 8:36).

Jesus Liberates
Of course, you can be freed, for example, from smoking. There are hundreds of avenues you can take to rid yourself of that habit. You can even sign up for a program that puts you in a hospital. Under careful medical guidance you will be helped

and perhaps finally freed of the addiction. But what's wrong with simply telling Jesus that you want to get rid of that filthy habit? Why not tell Jesus that you want to be free of the addiction of nicotine, free from impure thoughts, free from lying, free from gossiping? Simply go down to your knees, repent of that sin, and thank Him that He has cleansed you with His own precious blood. He has paid the price for your sins already, and you can receive total and absolute liberty from any oppression or depression. At this very moment, you can be free forever!

The Word of God is eternally valid, but we must be willing to come to the light. The Bible says, *"But if we walk in the light, as he is in the light, we have fellowship one with another, and the blood of Jesus Christ his Son cleanseth us from all sin"* (1st John 1:7). Please note the verse does not say from certain sins, for a limited time, but from "all sin." Verse 9 gives us the absolute guarantee, *"If we confess our sins, he is faithful and just to forgive us our sins, and to cleanse us from all unrighteousness."*

CHAPTER 8

Mystery Babylon Identified

Summary

The Bible clearly speaks of two entities: The "city" and the "whore." Religious deception and political democracy are shown in their proper relationship to the fulfillment of endtime Bible prophecy.

A four-fold criteria identifies Mystery Babylon. We also learn how the Roman system, through Europe, will unify this world politically, economically, and religiously. The process is underway right now.

Mystery Babylon Identified

There is a 4-fold criteria which helps us to identify Mystery Babylon.

First, Martyrs of Jesus. *"And I saw the woman drunken with the blood of the saints, and with the blood of the martyrs of Jesus: and when I saw her, I wondered with great admiration"* (Revelation 17:6). Surely there is no city in the world where *"...the blood of the martyrs of Jesus..."* was shed more so than in Rome. Persecution of Christians became a national sport. Huge crowds cheered as lions ripped the Christians to shreds.

This very first sign of identification removes all the cities of the world from consideration except Jerusalem.

John, who saw Mystery Babylon, was completely surprised. One translation says he *"...was astonished with great astonishment."* He saw something that was totally contrary to what he had ever seen before or ever imagined. He came face to face with the endtime climax of evil, *"...the mother of harlots and abominations of the earth..."* (verse 5). John saw more details than Daniel had seen over five centuries earlier!

Daniel Saw "Mystery Babylon"

In Daniel's case, we read of the last world empire, *"After this I saw in the night visions, and behold a fourth beast, dreadful and terrible, and strong exceedingly; and it had great iron teeth: it devoured and brake in pieces, and stamped the residue with the feet of it: and it was diverse from all the beasts that were before it; and it had ten horns"* (Daniel 7:7).

Daniel also was astonished beyond measure. He inquired about this fourth beast in verse 19, *"Then I would know the truth of the fourth beast, which was diverse from all the others, exceeding dreadful...."*

He received the answer in verse 23: *"The fourth beast shall be the fourth kingdom upon earth, which shall be diverse from all kingdoms, and shall devour the whole earth, and shall tread it down, and break it in pieces."*

John saw additional details. But he, too, had a problem and expressed his need for help: *"And the angel said unto me, Wherefore didst thou marvel? I will tell thee the mystery of the woman, and of the beast that carrieth her, which hath the seven heads and ten horns"* (Revelation 17:7). Two identities are being revealed: The woman and the beast. Now comes the explanation beginning in verse 8, *"The beast that thou sawest was, and is not; and shall ascend out of the bottomless pit, and go into perdition: and they that dwell on the earth shall wonder, whose names were not written in the book of life from the foundation of the world, when they behold the beast that was, and is not, and yet is."*

It's important to point out that John saw the *future* in the form of the *present*. He was in heaven in the Spirit, *"...come up hither...."* Revelation 4:2 says, *"...immediately, I was in the spirit...."* Therefore, John could describe these events for us from heavenly perspectives.

He confirmed Revelation 13:3, that all the Earth would "wonder after" the beast. One sense of the Greek for the word, "wonder" in Revelation 13:13 is that all the world is so *astounded* that they are actually driven *insane* by this beast!

A modern metaphor for this would be the *pandemonium* that breaks out when a rock group takes the stage. Tens of thousands of people go wild, actually go out of character, as their heroes strut out before them. Each individual becomes one with the sea of humanity glorifying the rock idols as the "music" begins.

Second, The Seven Hills. In Revelation 17:9, we have the second sign of identification, *"And here is the mind which hath wisdom. The seven heads are seven mountains, on which the woman sitteth."* From verse 18, we know that the woman is a city, *"And the woman which thou sawest is that great city, which reigneth over the kings of the earth."* Thus, Mystery Babylon must be a city geographically identifiable, and built on seven hills. No other city prides itself as the city on seven hills than does Rome.

Also, the angel does not fail to specifically emphasize that world unity is a coming reality in conjunction with this city, *"These have one mind, and shall give their power and strength unto the beast"* (verse 13). In verse 15, we have the explanation of verse 1 regarding the woman sitting upon many waters. *"And he saith unto me, The waters which thou sawest, where the whore sitteth, are peoples, and multitudes, and nations, and tongues."* This reinforces the interpretation that the last world system, which originates in Rome, will rule over the nations of this world.

Third, the Kings of the Earth. To discover the third point of identification, we must read Revelation 18:3, *"For all nations have drunk of the wine of the wrath of her fornication, and the kings of the earth have committed fornication with her, and the merchants of the earth are waxed rich through the abundance of her delicacies."*

There is no other city in the world which can claim special relationship with global political leaders, yet being in nature strictly religious. Only Rome with its nation-city, the Vatican, qualifies!

We have already discussed the result of the intoxication by wine in chapter 7 and emphasized that all the nations of the Earth with their government leaders will commit fornication with her.

Daniel Confirms
As a result of this fornicating relationship with global political leaders, a strong economy is created that makes the people on

Earth rich in abundance. Daniel confirms this prophetically: *"And in the latter time of their kingdom, when the transgressors are come to the full, a king of fierce countenance, and understanding dark sentences, shall stand up. And his power shall be mighty, but not by his own power: and he shall destroy wonderfully, and shall prosper, and practise, and shall destroy the mighty and the holy people.*

"And through his policy also he shall cause craft to prosper in his hand; and he shall magnify himself in his heart, and by peace shall destroy many: he shall also stand up against the Prince of princes; but he shall be broken without hand" (Daniel 8:23–25).

Reading the books of Daniel and Revelation allows us to see with clarity how this new, last world empire is being established. Geographically, it originates in a city which is built on seven hills, in which "the blood of the martyrs" was shed, out of which shall come a man who will be extremely successful.

Occult Deception

Daniel describes a "king" who will arise with the unique ability to understand "dark sentences." This is the occult. Daniel also reveals the secret of his understanding: The power will not be the king's, but as Revelation 13 clarifies, it is *given* to him by the dragon. This man shall do great and mighty things, *"...and shall prosper."* Luther translates this *"...through his wisdom, he shall be successful with his deception."* No doubt, he will be the most successful man on Earth. When he has reached that point, he will make the fatal mistake. He will permit blatant pride to take hold of him to such an extent that he will literally declare war against the God of heaven!

Fourth, A City on Fire, Visible From the Mediterranean. The fourth sign of identification is found in Revelation 18. After *"...her sins have reached unto heaven..."* (verse 5) God remembers her iniquity, *"...and she shall be utterly burned with fire..."* (verse 8). When that has happened, we see that the kings of the Earth, meaning the political elite of the world, and *"...the merchants of the earth..."* being the economic system, plus, *"...all the company in ships, and sailors, and as many as trade by sea, stood afar off"* (verse 17) *"...cried when they saw the smoke of her burning, saying, What city is like unto this great city!"* (verse 18). That means the whole world will be rocked by the destruction of Mystery Babylon, and the smoke rising from this city will be seen from the great sea, the Mediterranean.

Only Rome Qualifies
Let us summarize: To qualify for this horrible title, "Mystery Babylon," this city must not only have shed the blood of the martyrs of Jesus, be located on seven hills, and commit polit-ical-religious fornication with the leaders of the world, but it must also be seen, when on fire, from the sea. There is no other city on the face of the Earth that fits the four-fold criteria men-tioned. Only Rome qualifies.

Throughout church history, men of God have identified the Roman system as the Antichrist system.

Furthermore, it is the only city in the world within which there is a recognized nation. That is the Vatican. Many people fail to understand that the Vatican, the headquarters of the Catholic Church, is not only a religious organization, but is an established political state recognized by virtually all nations of the world including the prestigious United Nations.

Rome's Success
Today, we are seeing the continuous growth of the European Union which was founded on the doctrine of Rome.

For example, it is of interest that every president of the United States, although an overwhelmingly Protestant country, is received for an audience with the pope in the Vatican. Surely if both leaders of both nations are equal, then they can meet on equal footing. That, however, is not the case. An audience is something that is granted to a subject which is lower than the one giving the audience. Thereby, the leaders of the United States have literally committed fornication with this religious political figurehead who claims to be the sole legitimate representative of Christ of Earth, contrary to the clear teaching of the Bible.

Catholicism presents a great problem for fundamental Bible believers and vice-versa. A newspaper article clearly demonstrated this struggle:

> A new Vatican document on how to interpret the Bible condemns the fundamentalist approach as distorting and possibly leading to racism. The 130-page document... is the Roman Catholic Church's latest commentary on trends in Biblical study. Some of its language is unusually harsh, reflecting the challenge that fundamentalists pose to the church.
>
> "Without saying as much, in so many words, fundamentalism actually invites people to intellectual suicide," says the document from the Pontifical Biblical Commission. The authors save their harshest language for Christian fundamentalist denominations, which have been posing a challenge to the Roman church, particularly in Latin America... "The fundamentalist approach is dangerous, for it is attractive to people who look to the Bible for ready answers to the problems of life." [16]
>
> —The State, March 19, 1994, p.D8

Rome Versus Scripture
To read such an article in our daily newspaper shows the effectiveness of Bible-believing missionary activity.

The brutal and oppressive language the Vatican uses in this report reveals her great fear of losing her stranglehold on hundreds of millions who are led astray by her false doctrines such as the pope's infallibility, purgatory, the Eucharist, the rosary, the worship of the dead, worship of Mary, plus other cultic religious activities that are contrary to the precious Word of God.

Vatican doctrine, at the zenith of its visible wickedness, led to the sale of "indulgences," that is, the forgiveness of sins through the payment of money to the Roman treasury.

Yes, indeed, the fundamentalist (Bible) approach is dangerous to the Vatican, because it can liberate lost souls from the bondage of a manmade religion and lead them to the liberty in Jesus Christ through the preaching of the Gospel.

Rome Uniting Religions

We also know of the activity of Pope John Paul II regarding the uniting of all religions. The aim has not been just to have all Protestant churches unite under the World Council of Churches and then under the Roman Catholic Church. The intention goes much further, actually striving to unify ALL of the world's religions under the Roman umbrella. All nations and their religions must be united into one in order to fulfill Biblical prophecy, *"And all that dwell upon the earth shall worship him..."* (Revelation 13:8). In *Global Peace and the Rise of Antichrist*, Dave Hunt writes on page 129,

> The entire May/June 1988 issue of *The Catholic World* was devoted to Buddhism. The articles were all sympathetic, including favorable quotes from the pope. One article was even titled "The Buddha Revered As A Christian Saint"! John Paul II takes a broad-minded view of Buddhism and all other religions. He considers the Tibetan Buddhist Deity Yoga of his good friend the Dalai Lama, along with the prayers of witch doctors, spiritists, and every other "faith" to be generating

profound spiritual energies that are creating a new climate of
peace.

...Pope John Paul II slipped off his shoes to sit quietly and
solemnly with the supreme patriarch of Thailand's Buddhists
at a Buddhist monastery in Bangkok.... The Roman Catholic
pontiff later praised the ancient and venerable wisdom of the
Asian religion. [17]

Unifying Power of Babylon

Mystery Babylon is the religious power of the last world
empire, and for the first time in history, it can be realized. It is
not a power, however, that is based on a brutal oppressive
military force. It is a system that is supported voluntarily by
people the world over.

No one can deny that democracy, for example, has become
the god of politics. Woe unto any nation that refuses to implement democracy. While there are still rebels here and there, in
the long run, it will be impossible to withstand this new democratic world power structure that is even now beginning to
sweep over the world. Already, many nations are being punished by the U.N. for not implementing democracy.

It was impossible for the United States, for example, to
reject NAFTA [North American Free Trade Agreement] or the
GATT [General Agreement on Tariffs and Trade] treaties.
These and other trade agreements that will follow are only part
of the process that will lead the world into a virtually perfect
union. Finally, men will believe that they have achieved—with
their own power and free will—peace, stability, and prosperity as never before enjoyed in history.

People of the world will not need to be forced to worship,
praise, and *wonder* after the beast. They will *voluntarily* want
to be part of this new world order system and will enthusiasti-
cally worship the beast and his image.

Worldwide Babylon

The power of Mystery Babylon, although spiritually head-quartered in Rome, will not be isolated to that geographical city. As we have seen, it will be worldwide.

When we analyze European history, we quickly note that only Europe has affected the entire world. The Chinese did not go to Africa and establish colonies. Neither did the Africans go to America and conquer land. Nor did American Indians go to Asia or Europe and establish their dominance. Only Europe, this small continent, was able to subdue virtually the entire world. This is due to the power of the Roman system.

After many wars, especially two World Wars, Europe has learned that unity will not be achieved through weapons. Thus, we saw the fervent progress towards a unified Europe by means of political and financial policy. While it seemed like a utopian dream only 25 years ago, that is no longer the case today. The European Union is such a reality that the question of its existence is no longer valid, but today the big question is, "When will more nations be accepted into the European Union?" The more the union grows, the more nations will try to become part of it.

Ten Horns and Kings

We have already dealt with Revelation 13, looking at the Antichrist, Satan, the false prophet, and the image of the beast. But it seems necessary to point out a much misunderstood Scripture, of which Daniel also speaks of, namely, the beast *"...having seven heads and ten horns, and upon his horns ten crowns..."* (verse 1).

It is our understanding, based on the prophetic Word, that the ten horns—which are ten kings, mentioned in Revelation 17:12—are not representative of ten European nations, but rather ten different power structures. It is unrealistic to assume that North America, for example, would become a full-fledged

member of the European Union because of its geographic location. Therefore, an allied power structure will be established in
various parts of the world, but all under the leadership of the
European Union.

Just as the Roman European civilization has conquered the
world, the new system now being established will equally conquer the world, not by military force, but rather through a political, religious and economic system superior to all others.

Someone may now ask, "Did Europe really conquer the
world?" My answer is, "Absolutely yes!" While there is no
question about Europe and European-cultured continents such
as America and Australia, we know that Africa and Asia
equally must follow in the footsteps of Roman civilization in
order to compete in a modern world.

China has no chance to be part of the world's economy
unless they act "European," that is, to dress, communicate, and
govern according to the Roman model.

You don't see any Africans, for example, involved in any
business dealings the world over, using their own cultural
methods. The entire political-economic system is based on the
European Roman model.

While history records that in Asia, a sophisticated variety of
cultures did exist, the Chinese, Japanese, and others today use
business methods and communication that is fundamentally
European.

Europe Will Lead
Some may still doubt that the new world order system now
being established through the European Union is to rule the
world. But I am convinced that in a few years, there will no
longer be any doubt. It is evident, at least on the financial level
at this point, that Europe has superseded the United States.
America no longer is the nation that can dictate the financial
and economic structure of the world as in the past.

Such developments, however, are necessary for the prophetic Word to be fulfilled.

Not only Europe, but the entire world must follow the pattern of the European Roman civilization. Even the world's most populated nation, China, presently ruled by the communist system, is slowly but surely patterning itself after the European Roman system. The following news article shows with clarity how China is on the road to Rome:

> Persistence pays. That's what the European Union is finding in negotiations with Asia.
>
> Almost 10 months of painstaking negotiations have resolved a long-standing conflict over China's $2 billion in silk, linen and exports to the E.U. market.
>
> Big increases in import quotas by the E.U. have mollified the Chinese and muted protests by European importers.
>
> At the same time, the E.U. won Chinese agreement to cooperate on new E.U.-wide restrictions.
>
> Officials say all three agreements concluded on January 20—covering almost $9-billion worth of E.U. trade in textiles and clothing—were thrashed out without too much acrimony. It was a question of persistence rather than threats, says an E.U. trade official.[18]
>
> —Far Eastern Economic Review, February 2, 1995, p.52

During the last four decades, we have witnessed the almost breathtaking changes between Europe and the U.S.A..

Forty years ago, there was no question in anyone's mind regarding America's superiority. Today that is no longer true. America is dependent upon Europe more and more.

This is the progressive fulfillment of Bible prophecy which documents that all the nations of the Earth will be united through the "fornicating power" of the European system identified in Scripture as Mystery Babylon.

Final Rebellion

What, then, is the real purpose of Mystery Babylon and her world? It is the final rebellion of Satanic forces against the living God and His anointed. Psalm 2 makes this very plain, *"Why do the heathen rage, and the people imagine a vain thing? The kings of the earth set themselves, and the rulers take counsel together, against the LORD, and against his anointed, saying, Let us break their bands asunder, and cast away their cords from us"* (Psalms 2:1–3). This is precisely what is beginning to happen. The world is coming together, not necessarily for the purpose of destroying communism, dictatorship, or some other system. But the real reason for mankind's gathering is ultimately to oppose Him, the Creator of heaven and Earth. They will firmly declare "No!" to His Son, the Anointed One, through whom alone there is eternal salvation, and genuine peace and prosperity.

The people of the world in this drunken state do not sense the intoxication, but will continue to protest, rebel, and build upon their own sin-darkened imaginations that are contrary to the Word of God.

The unity of the world under the Antichrist will become so strong, and they will be so deceived, that they will have the courage to actually make war against the Lamb, *"These shall make war with the Lamb, and the Lamb shall overcome them: for he is Lord of lords, and King of kings: and they that are with him are called, and chosen, and faithful"* (Revelation 17:14).

Avoiding the Deception That Will Sweep the World

Mystery Babylon is being progressively revealed in our day. Only those who keep themselves pure, through the Lord Jesus Christ, are able to see and understand that the Lord is about to come back for His church. The full potency of evil will be revealed the moment the Church of Jesus Christ is raptured.

Jesus said, *"Ye are the light of the world...."* The church is the hindering element for the full development of rebellion. The moment this "light" is taken out of the way, utter darkness and deception will prevail on Earth. Then the Devil can finally implement his full intention. We, however, are not ignorant of his devices and that is one more reason why we should continuously study the Holy Word of God regarding that which is to come.

I emphasize that this evil is being presented in such a positive way that if it were possible, even the elect would be deceived. The power of Mystery Babylon is deception: *"...for by thy sorceries were all nations deceived"* (Revelation 18:23).

Christians who believe in the Word of God know the end result. We rejoice in that which is to come: *"Therefore rejoice, ye heavens, and ye that dwell in them. Woe to the inhabiters of the earth and of the sea! for the devil is come down unto you, having great wrath, because he knoweth that he hath but a short time"* (Revelation 12:12).

CHAPTER 9

Europe in Prophecy

Summary

T he amazing resurrection of the Roman world empire is being made visible through the formation of the European Union. This chapter shows how previously successful nations will not be able to compete with the new Roman empire, but must become subject to the new political, economic, and religious power structure. The world's smallest continent, Europe, is the only one that meets the Bible's specifications for the revived Roman empire.

Europe In Prophecy
When reading the title of this chapter, Europe In Prophecy, some may ask, "Why not 'America In Prophecy,' or 'Africa In Prophecy,' or 'Asia In Prophecy'?" The answer is simple: The Bible concerns itself primarily with the coming of the Messiah to Israel. Therefore, the nations surrounding Israel and their relationship to the land of redemption are the focal point of Bible prophecy. Israel is the center of the three continents— Europe, Asia, and Africa. Asia is listed several times in the Bible and a number of African countries are also mentioned.

Egypt, for example, has great significance because Israel became a nation in Egypt, and after 430 years moved out towards the Promised Land. Also, the Lord Jesus was protected from the wrath of King Herod in the land of Egypt.

But, what about the great Turkish empire that ruled the entire Middle East, including Israel and Jerusalem? Or Britain? It used to be said that the sun never set on the British empire. Surely the U.S.A. can be considered a world power structure that has left a significant mark on the planet. Many other nations have also achieved great and mighty things. This cannot be denied. Nevertheless, these and other nations are not mentioned in relationship to Israel because they did not exist during the time of Jesus' first coming, or demonstrated no major significance during the time of Christ on Earth.

The center of political, economic and military activity during the time of Christ was not Jerusalem, but Rome. The power of the Roman empire was spread across most of what we know today as Europe, plus the Mediterranean countries including Jerusalem and the land of Israel.

Four Gentile Empires
This is why we can legitimately focus on "Europe In Prophecy." While history records mighty deeds of a number of different nations, the Bible recognizes only four gentile power

structures throughout history: Babylon, Medo-Persia, Greece, and Rome. Therefore, we must not permit our focus to be distracted from the main geographic location on Earth, Israel, and the greatest power structure ever, Europe.

Also, we do well to remember that America, North and South, most of Africa, and Australia are a political reality due to the power of Europe.

Daniel's View

The prophet Daniel gave us a remarkable view of the four gentile power structures. He was a captive in Babylon and yearned to be back home in Israel.

Surely his heart went out to Jerusalem and the temple which, during his time, were destroyed. But there in a foreign land, God used Daniel to show us the whole power structure of the gentile nations from the beginning to the very end.

Babylon

King Nebuchadnezzar was the supreme ruler of Babylon, the first gentile world empire mentioned in the Bible.

The unfolding of the prophetic Word begins with his dream. After Nebuchadnezzar awoke, he could not recall the details. Immediately he called upon his intelligence advisors, the prognosticators, the think-tank of that time,

"Then the king commanded to call the magicians, and the astrologers, and the sorcerers, and the Chaldeans, for to shew the king his dreams. So they came and stood before the king" (Daniel 2:2).

After they heard the facts—that the king had a dream, but did now know the content—they confessed that they were powerless to describe or interpret it, *"And it is a rare thing that the king requireth, and there is none other that can shew it before the king, except the gods, whose dwelling is not with flesh"* (Daniel 2:11).

This is equally true today. The politicians, the intellectuals, the leaders of the world, and the news media are in total darkness when it comes to knowing the future. We must, therefore, consult Him who has the future in His hand. *"...Ask me of things to come..."* He invites us in Isaiah 45:11.

Nebuchadnezzar's Dream

No one was able to describe the details of the king's dream, subsequently, no one could interpret it. Then, the young Jewish man, Daniel, came on the scene, being summoned by Nebuchadnezzar. Here is what he says, *"Thou, O king, sawest, and behold a great image. This great image, whose brightness was excellent, stood before thee; and the form thereof was terrible. This image's head was of fine gold, his breast and his arms of silver, his belly and his thighs of brass,*

"His legs of iron, his feet part of iron and part of clay. Thou sawest till that a stone was cut out without hands, which smote the image upon his feet that were of iron and clay, and brake them to pieces.

"Then was the iron, the clay, the brass, the silver, and the gold, broken to pieces together, and became like the chaff of the summer threshingfloors; and the wind carried them away, that no place was found for them: and the stone that smote the image became a great mountain, and filled the whole earth" (Daniel 2:31–35).

How Europe is Arising to Assume Leadership

We see that the end result of the power structure of the nations is destruction. No nation, no matter how small or great, has a future on its own merits. Not even the renewed Roman empire has a positive future, ultimately. But as prophesied in Daniel, Rome will be a major power structure with links to Israel.

Officials in the Israeli government have in recent years praised the European Union, and expressed hopes that it will play a significant role in the peace process. Take the following comments made by former Israeli Prime Minister Shimon Peres a few years ago:

> "I believe that the role of EC in restructuring the new Middle East is major and essential," he said during a press conference with European President Jacques Delors. The European Community has pledged hundreds of millions of dollars of aid for Palestinians if Israel will relinquish territory in the West Bank, Gaza and Golan Heights. [19]
>
> —Wire reports, November 26, 1993

With this statement, Peres exposed to the world the E.U.'s real intention, namely, the surrender of Promised Land territory in exchange for negotiated peace.

Gold, Silver, Brass and Iron

Daniel interpreted the dream for Nebuchadnezzar, king of the Babylonian empire, and we can read the details as follows: *"Thou, O king, art a king of kings: for the God of heaven hath given thee a kingdom, power, and strength, and glory. And wheresoever the children of men dwell, the beasts of the field and the fowls of the heaven hath he given into thine hand, and hath made thee ruler over them all. Thou art this head of gold.*

"And after thee shall arise another kingdom inferior to thee, and another third kingdom of brass, which shall bear rule over all the earth. And the fourth kingdom shall be strong as iron: forasmuch as iron breaketh in pieces and subdueth all things: and as iron that breaketh all these, shall it break in pieces and bruise.

"And whereas thou sawest the feet and toes, part of potters' clay, and part of iron, the kingdom shall be divided; but there shall be in it of the strength of the iron, forasmuch as thou sawest the iron mixed with miry clay. And as the toes of the feet

were part of iron, and part of clay, so the kingdom shall be
partly strong, and partly broken.

"And whereas thou sawest iron mixed with miry clay, they
shall mingle themselves with the seed of men: but they shall not
cleave one to another, even as iron is not mixed with clay. And
in the days of these kings shall the God of heaven set up a king-
dom, which shall never be destroyed: and the kingdom shall
not be left to other people, but it shall break in pieces and con-
sume all these kingdoms, and it shall stand for ever.

"Forasmuch as thou sawest that the stone was cut out of the
mountain without hands, and that it brake in pieces the iron,
the brass, the clay, the silver, and the gold; the great God hath
made known to the king what shall come to pass hereafter: and
the dream is certain, and the interpretation thereof sure"
(Daniel 2:37–45).

We notice that the description does not start with the feet
going up to the head, but with the head going down to the feet.
In other words, the best first and the worst last, *"Thou, O king,*
art a king of kings..." (verse 37), *"...Thou art this head of*
gold" (verse 38).

Thus, the absolute superiority of King Nebuchadnezzar is
evident by the components of this image: First gold, then silver, after that, brass, and finally iron and clay. These four
empires are clearly identified and there is no question among
most Bible scholars regarding who they are:

Gold . . . . Babylon
Silver. . . . . Medo-Persia
Brass . . . . Greece
Iron . . . . Rome

The most significant of the four is the last one, the Iron empire.
The Prophet Daniel talks more about this last one than the three
previous ones together.

The Mystery of the "Iron and Clay"

Also extremely significant is the fact that a *fifth* component is added. To the iron is added clay. But this clay was not part of the iron empire from the beginning. We don't find the clay mixed with the iron in the legs, but only in the feet and the toes.

Although this is one empire, there is definitely a significant change in the end. This, no doubt, is the extension or resurrection of that empire.

Whereas the beginning of the fourth empire was of iron, and the *Pax Romana* policy was based on absolute military superiority, the last part of this empire still has the military strength of "iron," but clay is being added.

What does the clay stand for? I am convinced that the clay means the Jews. No doubt, the new world is a typical Jewish product, the leader of world democracy. I explain more about this on page 125.

Dictatorship Versus Democracy

When we compare this last empire, especially the last section of the last world empire, to the previous ones, we have to admit that the "iron-clay" mixture is of extremely poor quality. Actually, the two don't mix effectively at all.

Gold is very precious, while iron is available in abundance. Clay is even more available. When we think about these matters, we are shocked, because generally speaking, we reject, even condemn dictatorships and praise our democratic system.

In the language of democracy, the king of Babylon is described as a brutal oppressive dictator under whom the people suffered greatly. In contrast, democracy is considered to be the final liberty of mankind. We think highly of democracy because "we the people" are in charge.

We vote leaders into office who will rule us according to our laws which we have coined according to our preferences. This type of government could not have come into being during the time of the Romans because the practice of democracy was limited to the upper class. They still ruled their own land and those they had conquered with "a rod of iron."

Communism and the Jews

The first major change took place in 1848 when Karl Marx and Frederick Engels published the *Communist Manifesto*. Not surprisingly, the Jews were the first to promote this system because it promised them a chance to be equal to others. This was the first major attempt in modern times for the Jews to be integrated with the gentiles. Later, communism was taken over by an elite, vehemently antisemitic leadership, which resulted in great persecution of the Jews. Thus, instead of liberty, they experienced severe oppression.

Communism: Anti-Religion

A major reason for this was that the Jews were a religious people, whether they confessed it or not. Communism, however, rejected all types of religion and called it "the opium of the people." Thus, the Jewish drive for freedom and equality developed more successfully in the new world, primarily in the U.S.A.. Religious freedom was guaranteed and democracy was not only in the stage of being established in the United States but often exported to other nations. The progress of democracy eventually became the death sentence for communism.

Democracy Rules

Today, there is no longer a question regarding which system is superior. It is indisputably democracy. Now we are witnessing how, almost on a daily basis under this system of democracy, the world is becoming one. This is absolutely necessary, for the nations of this world must be united in order to fulfill Bible prophecy which tells us that *"...these have one mind..."* (Revelation 17:13) in the endtimes.

In order to facilitate this one-minded union, men are working feverishly to communicate better.

An article in *Popular Science* magazine shows how men want to reverse the effect of the Tower of Babel:

REVERSAL OF THE TOWER OF BABEL

Once a language interpreter and now a computer scientist, Hiraaki Kitano dreams of a machine that combines elements of both disciplines: A handheld computer and speech translator that could knock down the language barriers once and for all. Speak English words into the computer, for example, and out will come the same words spoken aloud in Spanish, French, or Japanese.

While electronic translators exist in limited form today, none of them use the kind of highly sophisticated voice-recognition and text-to-speech technology that would be needed to perform real-time bilingual exchanges quickly and accurately. At Carnegie Mellon University in Pittsburgh, Kitano is using a supercomputer and a separate device for voice recognition and voice synthesis to develop a new speech-to-speech translating system.[20]

—Popular Science, January 1994

There is no doubt that men will attain their goal, which is the eradication of the result of the Tower of Babel, the advent of many languages. It was the Lord God who confused the one world language in order to separate the various tribes of people. Genesis 11:6 reads, *"And the LORD said, Behold, the people is one, and they have all one language; and this they begin to do: and now nothing will be restrained from them, which they have imagined to do."*

The process toward a one world language does not need to be a language by itself, but rather the elimination of the hindrances to understanding each other. Eventually it will come

about by this new speech-to-speech system employing artifi-
cial intelligence software.

Lion, Bear, Leopard—Dreadful and Terrible

As we mentioned previously, the last kingdom is an extension
of the fourth kingdom, but is slightly different. The iron-clay
kingdom is definitely diverse. It has different characteristics,
being the only government that mixes two components.

Later in Daniel 7, the prophet passes on additional information he received to reinforce that the final kingdom will be
diverse from all the others, *"Daniel spake and said, I saw in
my vision by night, and, behold, the four winds of the heaven
strove upon the great sea. And four great beasts came up from
the sea, diverse one from another.*

*"The first was like a lion, and had eagle's wings: I beheld
till the wings thereof were plucked, and it was lifted up from the
earth, and made stand upon the feet as a man, and a man's
heart was given to it.*

*"And behold another beast, a second, like to a bear, and it
raised up itself on one side, and it had three ribs in the mouth
of it between the teeth of it: and they said thus unto it, Arise,
devour much flesh.*

*"After this I beheld, and lo another, like a leopard, which
had upon the back of it four wings of a fowl; the beast had also
four heads; and dominion was given to it.*

*"After this I saw in the night visions, and behold a fourth
beast, dreadful and terrible, and strong exceedingly; and it had
great iron teeth: it devoured and brake in pieces, and stamped
the residue with the feet of it: and it was diverse from all the
beasts that were before it; and it had ten horns"* (Daniel
7:2–7).

What is so striking here again is the fact that the first three
empires can be easily identified: A lion, a bear, and a leopard.
But the fourth beast cannot be named, or described as having

the characteristics of any existing animal. It is completely diverse.

"What's Wrong With Democracy?"

At this point, the reader may ask, "What's wrong with democracy?" This is exactly what Patti Lalonde wrote to me after proofreading this chapter. She said,

> Today the nations of the world are mostly democratic. Democracy hasn't seemed so bad. I'm glad I was born in a democratic nation rather than a communist one or a dictatorship. What is so terrible about democracy?

Indeed, there is nothing wrong with democracy. It guarantees more freedom, justice, and pursuit of happiness for the individual than under any other system.

However, to believe in democracy to the extent that one is convinced the world will live in peace and harmony under it is where the great deception comes in.

Therefore, when we look at democracy in a critical light, we need not search for hidden diabolical evils that will come forth or bring about the rulership of the Antichrist, but rather the normal activity of eating and drinking, marrying and giving in marriage, buying and selling, or planting and building.

But in the success thereof lies the great deception.

The Time of Noah

Let's look at a scriptural example. Luke 17:26–27 reads, *"And as it was in the days of Noe, so shall it be also in the days of the Son of man.*

"They did eat, they drank, they married wives, they were given in marriage, until the day that Noe entered into the ark, and the flood came, and destroyed them all."

No particular sin is mentioned here, but simply the normal day-to-day activity. We still eat and drink, we marry and give into marriage.

Nothing has changed since the day of Noah in regard to human behavior. As believers in Jesus, we do likewise, but there is a distinct difference.

While living our lives as described above, we are preparing for the coming of the Lord, *"Looking for that blessed hope, and the glorious appearing of the great God and our Saviour Jesus Christ"* (Titus 2:13).

Lot and Sodom

Jesus also compared His second coming with the time of Lot, *"Likewise also as it was in the days of Lot; they did eat, they drank, they bought, they sold, they planted, they builded; But the same day that Lot went out of Sodom it rained fire and brimstone from heaven, and destroyed them all.*

"Even thus shall it be in the day when the Son of man is revealed" (Luke 17:28–30).

Again, we see the Lord enumerated the normal day-to-day activity of people, and again, He emphasized, *"...thus shall it be in the day when the Son of man is revealed."*

The days of Noah and the days of Lot are given to us by our Lord Jesus as signs of the most terrible day that is yet to come, which we call the Great Tribulation.

It is in vain, therefore, to endlessly look for some hidden political agenda or conspiracy by the bankers and leaders of this world.

Rather, we are instructed to look at the normal day-to-day activity in which people place their hope on a better world, more righteousness, peace, and prosperity, *without* the Prince of Peace, the Lord Jesus Christ.

To identify this final kingdom in prophecy, we are required to analyze a new political system and pinpoint a philosophy that is incomparable with any others in the history of mankind. Such a system and philosophy is being developed today in Europe.

Europe Today

Not only is the European Union uniting geographically through economics and politics, but the unthinkable is also taking place today: They are uniting religiously as well. The most diverse continent is unifying!

Furthermore, Europe is looking to the East to prepare former communist countries for integration into the European Union!

The original Roman empire would have done this by force. Now it's being accomplished peacefully through democracy.

The *Daily Mail* of April 2, 1994 reported:

> Hungary was the FIRST FORMER COMMUNIST BLOC COUNTRY to apply to join the European Union, saying it needed membership to "GUARANTEE SECURITY AND INTEGRITY." Hungary's bid to move into the western economic system is likely to be followed this month by Poland and later by the Czech Republic. [21]

Here we have an excellent example of democracy moving eastward, instead of communism moving westward, as has been the fear for decades. Since communism has declined, there is only ONE alternative: Social-capital democracy!

The realization that democracy is the key to the new world order, which opens the door for Satan to install the Antichrist as its head, really hits us hard.

Concerning governments, we have been taught in schools, churches, and universities that the liberty of the world can only come about when men can choose leaders under a system of democracy.

The Praises of Democracy

Quite often I have heard believers pray in their church and praise God for the "free government of democracy." I wish to make myself clear: My choice, too, is democracy. This is not a statement from someone who has been taught that democracy is best, but I personally have experienced a great deal of suffering through National Socialism and communism. I know what it means because I was there!

I would be guilty, however, if I were to hide the Biblically prophesied reality that when men rule themselves and do as they please, which is increasingly the case now, the result will lead to the greatest catastrophe the world has ever known.

Three Endtime Proofs

Someone may now ask, "Are you sure the Bible speaks of democracy as the last gentile government?" Yes, I am absolutely sure, because it is the last world empire. How do I know it's the last one? Here are three central reasons:

First, the Jews are going back to the land of Israel:
"And I will bring them out from the people, and gather them from the countries, and will bring them to their own land, and feed them upon the mountains of Israel by the rivers, and in all the inhabited places of the country" (Ezekiel 34:13).

Second, the land has been resurrected from the dead:
"But ye, O mountains of Israel, ye shall shoot forth your branches, and yield your fruit to my people of Israel; for they are at hand to come" (Ezekiel 36:8).

Third, Jerusalem is a Jewish city after 2500 years:
"And in that day will I make Jerusalem a burdensome stone for all people: all that burden themselves with it shall be cut in pieces, though all the people of the earth be gathered together against it" (Zechariah 12:3).

God's Word says these things will happen before the Tribulation, the final seven years during which the new world order, dominated by the Roman European model, will exist as the final empire. The fulfillment of prophecy is the proof that we are living in the last times and therefore the system of government prevalent during those times must be the last one.

The Clay

We have established that the last world empire consists of a mixture between iron and clay. We showed that iron symbolizes the ancient Roman power structure. The clay, however, represents the power of the people, the idea embodied in the practice of democracy.

Wherever democracy has been practiced for generations, you will find a large number of Jews prospering.

I submit, therefore, that the clay represents the Jewish people, attempting to fully integrate into the new world order.

The Bible gives us a very clear answer as to who the clay represents: *"But now, O LORD, thou art our father; we are the clay, and thou our potter; and we all are the work of thy hand"* (Isaiah 64:8).

No other group of people has been integrated into the nations of the world to the extent the Jews have been. But, and this is a great miracle, they never lost their identity!

The Prussian king, Frederick the Great, once asked his advisor, "Give me proof that there is a God," and the advisor answered, "The Jews your majesty, the Jews!"

One does not need to do much research to find that in virtually all nations of the world, there at the center of success, you will find a group of Jews! Before 1948, the founding of the nation of Israel, the Jews had no political power in their own right.

They always were subject unto other nations. With the founding of the State of Israel, this changed dramatically. Israel has become a nation and has stood ground against an overwhelming majority of enemies.

Israel has been literally resurrected from an unproductive desert land to an agricultural powerhouse. From scratch, the Jews have established a military force second to none in the world. Actually, no air force in the world can match the skill of Israel's fighter pilots.

Although a brand new nation, she is no longer considered a developing one and is generously giving foreign aid to many countries.

The gross national product per capita is going to exceed that of the U.S. in just a few years. Israel is the modern day miracle! She is moving strongly into high-tech, a good sign for the future.

Today, more and more nations are establishing diplomatic and economic relations with Israel.

The Covenant of Rome With Israel

Reuter's news service wrote about Israel's covenant with the Vatican in a story filed on December 29, 1993:

> In a landmark step after 2,000 years of strained Christian-Jewish relations, Vatican and Israeli negotiators approved a document in which the Holy See and the Jewish state formally recognize one another. The document, the most important step in Israeli-Vatican relations since the Jewish state was founded in 1948, was given final approval by delegations which had worked on the accord for 17 months.
>
> Vatican spokesman Joaquin Navarro-Valls said the accord may make it easier for the Vatican to play a greater role in constructing Middle East peace. In the preamble, the Vatican and Israel agree on the singular significance of the Holy Land. [22]

Israel was intoxicated with joy when relations between the Vatican and Jerusalem were established. Shimon Peres made the following statement:

...This is an historic act. This is not only an agreement on the
establishment of relations between the Vatican and the State of
Israel, but it is also a change in the long, twisting, painful pattern of relations between two great religions—the Christian
and the Jewish...I hope a day will come when a third partner
will join this agreement: the Muslim partner. [23]

—Christians & Israel, Volume 3, No.1, Winter 1993/94, p.5

The Prize is Peace

Israel is willing to compromise. The prize is peace. The avenue
to achieve peace is negotiation. The price for Israel is giving
up large portions of the Promised Land and sovereignty over
Jerusalem. The end result: Peace for Israel and the Arab world
will explode the Middle East into a new powerhouse!

The Four World Empires Alive Today

It is of great interest that remnants of the four world empires
still exist today as identifiable entities. Even more significant
is the fact that all four have been involved in military conflicts
in recent decades.

Today's Iraq, for example, occupies the area of ancient
Babylon [the gold empire]. Persia [the silver empire] is modern-day Iran. These two nations were involved in a war that
lasted from 1980–1988. Greece [the bronze empire] warred
against Turkey in 1974 over the island of Cyprus. Even today,
there is still an ongoing tension between them. Rome [the iron
empire] was heavily involved during the Gulf conflict against
Iraq in 1991. Rome, identified in the Bible as "Mystery
Babylon," opposed the old Babylon [Iraq] in this war.

Rome Attacking Iraq?

Let me explain. What is the proof for our statement that Rome
was the force that went against Iraq? There are a number of
valid reasons:

First, the United States, which supplied the major military force, operated under the auspices of the United Nations. We must keep in mind that 87% of U.S. citizens are descendants of European immigrants, who in turn are descendants of the Romans.

Second, it was Europe [Rome] and Japan who paid for the war against Iraq. Literally speaking, American soldiers became Roman mercenaries.

I realize that this is a shocking statement to make, but based on international law, it is correct. If a soldier fights for the interest of another country and gets paid by another nation, he is considered a mercenary. American soldiers paid by Europe (Rome) fought for the interest of a third nation, which was Kuwait.

For the first time in modern history, we saw virtually all nations of the world unite against one nation, Babylon [Iraq]. Let's not overlook this important fact.

While it was an overt victory for the allied coalition over Iraq, for the State of Israel, the war ended too soon. The *Kansas City Star* carried this report on January 15th, 1995:

BUSH SHOCKED SHAMIR
Former Israeli Prime Minister Yitzhak Shamir said he and his cabinet ministers "almost fell off our chairs" when President Bush decided to end the 1991 Persian Gulf War before Iraqi leader Saddam Hussein was toppled. His air force commander described secret Israeli reconnaissance flights over Iraq, clandestine contacts with Jordan's King Hussein and tough bargaining with the Americans, who wanted to keep Israel out of the fighting at any price. [24]

Israel's intention was to eliminate the military threat of Iraq, but it did not happen. Again, foreign powers dictated Israel's course of action!

As we have just seen, remnants of all four gentile world empires exist today. They must be identifiable, otherwise, the prophecy of Daniel 2 cannot be fulfilled, for it specifically states that all four world empires, including the fifth, the iron-clay, are going to be destroyed by the stone, which is the Lord Jesus Christ. It stands to reason that you can't destroy something that does not exist.

Mystery Babylon in Jesus' Time

The prophetic Word points out that the same people who destroyed the city of Jerusalem and the sanctuary, the Jewish temple, will be in charge again when those things are restored. Let's read Daniel 9:26–27: *"And after threescore and two weeks shall Messiah be cut off, but not for himself: and the people of the prince that shall come shall destroy the city and the sanctuary; and the end thereof shall be with a flood, and unto the end of the war desolations are determined. And he shall confirm the covenant with many for one week: and in the midst of the week he shall cause the sacrifice and the oblation to cease, and for the overspreading of abominations he shall make it desolate, even until the consummation, and that determined shall be poured upon the desolate."*

Verse 26 describes history. The temple in Jerusalem was destroyed by *"...the people of the prince that shall come...."* The "people" who destroyed the temple and Jerusalem in A.D. 70 were the Romans. The "prince" is referring to the Antichrist, who will come in the future, from the revived Roman empire. It tells of a certain covenant that will be confirmed by the "prince" for a one week of years [7 years].

The *"...overspreading of abomination that makes desolate..."* has not taken place yet. It will occur during the Great Tribulation.

The Lord Jesus emphasizes this fact in Matthew 24:15, *"When ye therefore shall see the abomination of desolation,*

spoken of by Daniel the prophet, stand in the holy place...."
Thus, the same people must rule again when Christ comes
back. Rome ruled when Jesus came the first time, and Rome
must rule when Jesus comes back!

I venture to say, therefore, that Israel and the former Roman
Mediterranean countries will be accepted into the European
Union in the future. When this takes place, Europe (Rome) will
dominate world finances, world trade, world military policy,
and as always, world religion. And we must add, world energy
sources!

Mystery Babylon Not to Be Found in Iraq
We have already established in chapters seven and eight who
Mystery Babylon is. But we must reemphasize it again because
in recent years, a number of books have been written identifying New York City as Mystery Babylon. Others have pointed
out that Saddam Hussein was rebuilding some of the ruins of
the original Babylon. Interpretation was made that this is going
to be Mystery Babylon when completed. It was proposed that
the city will be reconstructed and become the most significant
city enabling it to establish world authority.

According to our understanding of Scripture, neither New
York City, Babylon in Iraq, or any other city except Rome
meets the Biblical description of "Mystery Babylon."

Let us read again Revelation 18:3, *"For all nations have
drunk of the wine of the wrath of her fornication, and the kings
of the earth have committed* **fornication** *with her, and the merchants of the earth are waxed rich through the abundance of
her delicacies."*

Here we have a very unique identification: The mixture
between politics and religion. The key word is "fornication."
The Greek for this word suggests harlotry, unlawful lust, or
idolatry. Here's the connection: In Rome, there was a vibrant
church. It was so dynamic that the Apostle Paul testified,

*"To all that be in Rome, beloved of God, called to be saints:
Grace to you and peace from God our Father, and the Lord
Jesus Christ. First, I thank my God through Jesus Christ for
you all, that your faith is spoken of throughout the whole
world"* (Romans 1:7–8). But in the year A.D. 324, the church
was *integrated* into the political system of Emperor
Constantine. Since then, the Roman church has committed
"fornication" with the kings and the merchants of the Earth!

Because the Church of Jesus Christ has no political mandate
given to it in the Word of God, and the Vatican is recognized
by the entire world as a political identity, we have the absolute
assurance that Rome, where once a true church was located, is
characterized in Revelation 18:3 as the one committing fornication with the kings of the Earth!

Meanwhile, how the Vatican is reaching for world religious
leadership can be seen from the following newspaper report:

Pope John Paul II spoke with warmth of his friendship for the
Jewish community and his respect for the Jewish faith, his
recognition of the right of Israel to exist, and the disturbing
memories from his youth in occupied Poland of the
Holocaust...His "greatest dream," he is telling friends and vis-
itors these days, is to go there (Jerusalem) on a religious pil-
grimage as soon as possible.

He had visited the Holy Land as a bishop more than 20
years ago, but a return to Jerusalem as pope has a crucial spiritual and peacemaking meaning for him. Israel has already
invited him for a state visit.

"We trust," the pope said, "that with the approach of the
year 2000, Jerusalem will become the city of peace for the
entire world and that all the people will be able to meet there,
in particular the believers in the religions that find their
birthright in the faith of Abraham."[25]

—The Herald, 4/4/94

While the pope's statement incorporates ecumenical religious
overtones, one cannot avoid detecting the political aim by his
emphasizing that "Jerusalem will become the city of peace for
the entire world."

We would make a great error by underestimating the deep
desire of the pope, the Vatican, the European Union, and Israel
for unity and peace at any cost.

CHAPTER 10

How Europe Will Lead the World

Summary

The amazing development of the European Union leads us to be convinced that, on the one hand, world communism will not be resurrected to the extent it was before 1991. On the other hand, we have indisputable evidence that the United States will loose its capitalistic leadership of the world. Thus, the door is open for Europe to lead the New World Order.

How Europe Will Lead the World

I would like to emphasize the phrase, *"These have one mind...."* Even today we are witness to the uniting of the nations, which will ultimately lead to the fulfillment of prophecy as described in the above verse. The most unity-seeking people in the world are the Europeans.

America, Picture of Unity

During the last 100 years, Europe has looked toward America with envy. Americans had better houses, bigger cars, more luxuries and the land was at peace. The dream of uniting Europe was resurrected over and again because of the "New World" example.

Although the population of the USA was overwhelmingly European, they were doing much better than their cousins in Europe. What was the reason? The answer can be found in the old adage, "United we stand, divided we fall."

The United "States" Never Really Became States

The original idea for the role of state and federal government never materialized, fortunately. The "states" never became sovereign states. Otherwise, America would have experienced similar problems as Europe.

Each state would have become an independent sovereign nation, with its own currency, independent laws, defined borders, and its own military force. One could well imagine that independent states would select the language and culture of the majority of the people who settled there, whether they were Italian, German, French, Spanish, Polish, Hungarian, or other ethnic groups. A duplicate of Europe would have been realized.

America was on its way to becoming a series of independent states, but the idea was crushed by the Civil War, which finally resulted in the solidifying of the nation as one. Instead of states in the truest sense, the U.S.A. became a group of provinces of Washington D.C., in reality without the rights of truly sovereign independent states.

Unity Only Through Peace, Not War

Europe, instead of uniting, was more divided than ever during the time of America's success. Two World Wars were fought, which did not help to unite the people. Following World War II, Eastern and Western Europe were divided because of communism.

But these world-shaking events changed the European consciousness. It was understood that peace and prosperity could not be established through military force.

After 2,000 years of conflicts, and watching the progress of the United States specifically since the beginning of the 1900's, the European spirit of unity was awakened.

The first step towards unity was the Treaty of Rome signed in 1957. At that beginning, proposals were made to cooperate on the level of trade and commerce and no indication was made at that time for further unity in any other way.

Europe: The Beginning of the Last Empire

Revelation 17:13–14 gives us a description of the rulership of the last gentile power structure, *"These have one mind, and shall give their power and strength unto the beast. These shall make war with the Lamb...."* To make war with the Lamb will require unity, a characteristic not historically attributed to Europe.

Later I will go into detail regarding the progressive development of the European Union, but right now, I want to emphasize the dynamic power of it in regard to the near future. Our local newspaper, *The State*, carried the following story on December 12, 1994:

Leaders of the 12 [now 15, for the meantime] European Union
nations agreed to begin open-ended discussions about membership for six Eastern European countries without setting a
timetable for any of them to join.

Top officials from all six European countries that now have
association agreements with the European Union—Poland, the
Czech Republic, Slovakia, Romania, Bulgaria and Hungary—
met with the leaders at the Villa Hugel. The European Union
said they hoped to include the six countries plus the three
Baltic republics and Slovenia in a series of studies and regular
meetings on how to prepare them for membership in the
world's largest trading and political cooperation group.... [26]

This, of course, is old news, but today we recognize, in unmistakable terms, the spirit of unity in Europe has become reality.

Why Europe Must Lead the World

Virtually all European nations can identify, in their history, that
their greatest glory was during the Roman world empire. That
empire, with all its power, wisdom, glory and culture, is
doubtlessly the center stage, not only of European history, but
literally the entire world.

Rome and Europe must be credited as the founders of the
world's westernized civilization, and the birth of democracy as
well. Today, democracy is the indisputable world ideology in
virtually all political systems. But Europe is the major influence on Western civilization.

1) It is the center of the world, lying between East
   and West.
2) It is the center of philosophy that has shaped
   the progressive civilization of the world.
3) It is the center of trade, commerce and
   finances.

4) It is the center and leader of religion in the world. There is no individual on Earth more powerful in religion, which directly affects politics, than the pope of Rome.

In South and Central America, for example, many nations do not permit anyone to be president unless he is Roman Catholic. Their cultures are virtually dominated by the philosophy of the Vatican.

It is important to emphasize that Rome is not limited to Europe. It is worldwide! When the pope travels the world, he draws crowds that dwarf any other individual, including top political leaders.

Millions hang on his every word. He is considered infallible, and his church claims that he is the only representative of Christ on Earth. Crowds bow at his feet and kiss his ring. They long to be touched and blessed by this icon in white flowing robes.

Europe Imitates Israel
I would like to point out here that these four characteristics were actually meant for Israel.

Israel is the center of the Earth:
1) *"Thus saith the Lord GOD; This is Jerusalem: I have set it in the midst of the nations and countries that are round about her"* (Ezekiel 5:5). Luther translates Ezekiel 38:12 as "Dwelling in the midst of the earth." And the Hebrew Bible reads: "Living at the center of the earth."

Israel is the center of wisdom. No one can compare with the wisdom of King Solomon:
2) *"And all the earth sought to Solomon, to hear his wisdom, which God had put in his heart"* (1st Kings 10:24).

Israel is to be the center of commerce and finances:

3) *"For the Lord thy God blesseth thee,* [Israel] *as he promised thee: and thou shalt lend unto many nations, but thou shalt not borrow; and thou shalt reign over many nations, but they shall not reign over thee"* (Deuteronomy 15:6).

Israel is the center of true religion:

4) *"And there was given him dominion, and glory, and a kingdom, that all people, nations, and languages, should serve him: his dominion is an everlasting dominion, which shall not pass away, and his kingdom that which shall not be destroyed"* (Daniel 7:14). This is referring to the reign of the Messiah in Israel, not the "prince" which will come from the revived Roman empire.

Europe Wants to Replace Israel

The prophetic shadow that is being cast shows that Europe (the new Roman empire), attempts to imitate Israel. It is therefore of no surprise that the flag of Europe contains twelve stars in a circle, and not fifteen, or whatever the final number of nations belonging to the European Union will be. Europe's constitution requires that only twelve stars should represent all nations that will be gathered into the Union. We don't need much imagination to see that the twelve stars imitate Israel in a two-fold way: First, the twelve tribes of the children of Israel, and second, the twelve apostles of the Lamb! As already mentioned, the spirit of Europe is not limited geographically to Europe. Let me explain:

The West

Over 500 years ago, the Roman Catholic Jew, Christopher Columbus, discovered America. The entire continent, (both north and south), was claimed by Spain in the name of the Roman church. The populations of the U.S.A., Canada, and the nations of South America, are made up mainly of European descendants.

Our governments are based on Roman principles. The supreme council of ancient Rome was called the Senate. This identical system is used today in the U.S.A., and Canada. This also applies to Italy, France, Ireland, South Africa, and Australia, just to name a few.

It is also obvious that government buildings throughout the U.S.A. are strikingly similar to the Roman architecture of the Vatican. Virtually all major government buildings are crowned with the cupola, the dome, just like St. Peter's Cathedral in Rome. So our history ties us to the Roman empire. And even though there has been a time of apparent separation, the West will return to its roots under the revived Roman empire.

The East
Australia has its roots in the European civilization as well. Ninety-two percent of its population is of European descent.

If we were to analyze the governments of Japan, Korea, Hong Kong, India, Taiwan, and other progressive Asian countries, we would find that they, too, are based on the principles of the Western European civilization.

The infrastructure of virtually all nations—be it government, education, transportation, communication, business transactions, laws, etcetera—are based on the European way of doing things.

India, the world's largest democracy, is a British creation. Although they have tried desperately to implement Hindi as their national language for many decades, English is still the language of communication in India. Indians whose mother tongue is not Hindi, but Bengali, Gujarat, Kashmiri, Telugu, Sanskit, and an additional 1652 dialects, refuse to accept Hindi as the national language of India. Thus, they must communicate in English!

The South
To the south of Rome lies Africa. Fifty percent of the continent
speaks French. Forty percent speak English. (Africa, too, is saturated with European civilization.) Therefore, Africa also
comes under the jurisdiction of the spirit of Rome.

Southern European countries see Africa as a neglected continent. E.U. members would like to see such African nations
brought into the fold somehow. Especially, Mediterranean
nations have long complained that the E.U. is facing the wrong
way.

They claim that while it focuses its attention on Eastern
Europe, a much greater threat looms from the south. Unless
Europe acts, they argue, Islamic fundamentalists will seize
power in the North African countries, unleashing a wave of
emigration. *The European* wrote in their March 9, 1995, issue:

> Will the southern governments succeed in persuading their
> northern E.U. partners to allocate more E.U. resources to the
> troubled Muslim nations of the Maghreb—Algeria, Morocco,
> Libya and Tunisia—across the new fault line that has replaced
> the Iron Curtain?
>
> Their aim is to persuade the E.U. to provide aid to develop
> industries in the Maghreb countries so that prosperity will
> reduce both emigration to Europe and support for fundamen-
> talism. [27]

More and more Europeans are recognizing their responsibility
and the danger of neglecting northern African nations. Islamic
fundamentalism has become one of the world's major security
risks, especially since the fall of the Soviet Union. But
Muslims will not adhere to any dictate. A religious compromise must be found. That can only be achieved through the
Vatican, the leader of the world's largest religion. Thus we see,
again, Rome and her influence worldwide!

Religion

If Europe is the center of the world for the gentiles, Italy is the center of Europe, with Rome the center of Italy and the Vatican the center of Rome.

The Vatican is world headquarters for the Catholic church and for Christianity (not Bible-believing). It appears that all major Christian denominations will sooner or later be integrated under the power structure of the Vatican. And indeed, Rome not only claims sole leadership of Christianity, it is becoming the indisputable leader of all other religions as well. How will this be accomplished? By accommodating other religions outside of Christianity such as Islam, Hinduism, Buddhism, and others. This type of "big umbrella" was typical of the spirit of Rome in ancient days as well. The idea was, "You may worship your own god, but in the name of Caesar."

Today the philosophy is being popularized that all people, regardless of what religion they adhere to, worship the one true God. They only use different names for their deities, but they all have a commonality in their faiths. Here's one example:

> Pope John Paul II slipped off his shoes to sit quietly and solemnly with the supreme patriarch of Thailand's Buddhists at a Buddhist monastery in Bangkok...The Roman Catholic pontiff later praised the "ancient and venerable wisdom" of the Asian religion. [28]
>
> —Courier Journal, May 11, 1984, p.A7

Pope John Paul II is not the only driving force behind ecumenism, of course. Newark Episcopalian Bishop John D. Spong wrote,

> In the fall of 1988, I worshiped God in a Buddhist temple. As the smell of incense filled the air, I knelt before three images of Buddha, feeling that the smoke could carry my prayers

heavenward. It was for me a holy moment...beyond the creeds
that each (religion) uses, there is a divine power that unites
us.... I will not make any further attempt to convert the
Buddhist, the Jew, the Hindu or the Moslem. I am content to
learn from them and to walk with them side by side toward the
God who lives, I believe, beyond the images that bind and
blind us. [29]

—The Voice, Diocese of Newark, January 1989

Speaking to Hindu audiences at the University of Calcutta,
Pope John Paul II noted,

India's mission is crucial, because of her intuition of the spiritual nature of man. Indeed, India's greatest contribution to the
world can be to offer it a spiritual vision of man. And the world
does well to attend willingly to this ancient wisdom and in it
to find enrichment for human living.

—L'Observatore Romano, February 10, 1986, p.5

I do believe we would be wasting paper to say more about the
intended unity of religions the world over under the leadership
of Rome.

Economy

In spite of severe difficulties and sometimes seemingly insur-
mountable obstacles, Europe is pressing towards full unity.
They are working to implement one currency. Borders are
being made increasingly transparent. Unity is the absolute key
word.

At this moment, Europe is already the economic leader of
the world. We must keep in mind that this is only the beginning. The fifteen nations that are now full members are not, it
appears, the complete European Union of the future. Many
more nations are waiting in line to become part of the Union.

This includes many Eastern European nations that want to join. For example, let me show you how desperate the eastern Mediterranean country of Turkey is to join the European Union. Former Prime Minister Tansu Ciller, interviewed by *The European*, said:

> It's very hard for my people to understand how countries which were in the communist bloc can move ahead of Turkey, which has a long association with the European Union and is a partner of NATO.
>
> —The European, 12/15/94, p.1

America In Deep Trouble
When it became clear that Europe was emerging as an economic superstate, America realized it had to make some dramatic moves to keep pace. It was for this reason that NAFTA (North American Free Trade Agreement) was passed so quickly. It joined Canada, the U.S. and Mexico into a common bond, trade-wise.

There have been many reports during the last two decades that indicate America is in deep trouble, with one of the major problems being our government's inability to balance the budget. In a few years, we are told, the government will not even be able to pay the interest on the national debt. It is borrowing on each new annual budget. This should not surprise us, for the old Anglo-American economic system must make room for the new hybrid European social/capital system.

We cannot deny the fact that our economy is becoming inferior to Europe's. No longer are the Americans dominating the financial boardrooms:

> Communism is dead and a new economic order is still to be discovered. The question of capitalism as opposed to the centrally-planned economy is that of private versus public interests

and corporation versus government. We are at the crossroads
of restructuring two conflicting forces. Three types of corporations are competing: The Anglo-American type based on
share-ownership; the Japanese type, which is heavily influenced by social considerations; and the European type, which
lies somewhere between the two.[32]

—The European, May 26, 1994, p.25

The Changing Times

When BMW, the German car manufacturer, was searching for
a "cheap labor nation" to locate an additional assembly plant,
they chose the U.S.A. (South Carolina). The superiority of the
Roman-European system was clearly demonstrated by the following fact: For one manufacturing hour in Germany, it costs
BMW $30. But in South Carolina, BMW pays only $12–$15
an hour. The U.S.A. is already a country where a cheap labor
force is available in abundance.

**Hourly Compensation Costs in
U.S. Dollars for Factory Workers:**

	1985	1995
Germany	$9.60	$31.88
Switzerland	9.66	29.28
Belgium	8.97	26.88
Austria	7.58	25.38
Finland	8.16	24.78
Norway	10.37	24.38
Denmark	8.13	24.19
Netherlands	8.75	24.18
Japan	6.34	23.66
Sweden	9.66	21.36
Luxembourg	7.72	20.06
France	7.52	19.34

UNITED STATES	**$13.01**	**$17.20**
Italy	7.63	16.48
Canada	10.94	16.03
Australia	8.20	14.40
Ireland	5.92	13.83
United Kingdom	6.27	13.77
Spain	4.66	12.70
Israel	4.06	10.59
New Zealand	4.47	10.11
Greece	3.66	8.95
Korea	1.23	7.40
Singapore	2.47	7.28
Taiwan	1.50	5.82
Portugal	1.53	5.35
Hong Kong	1.73	4.82
Mexico	1.59	1.51
Sri Lanka	.28	.45

(Note: Latest figures for Luxembourg and Sri Lanka are for 1994)

This does not mean that America is going "down the drain" as many continue to claim. The opposite is the truth. Today, the average American makes more money than ever before in history. He lives in a better house and the car he drives is an extremely superior product than the one from twenty-five years ago. We never have had such luxury and buying power for our hourly wage, in spite of some statistics that claim differently.

When analyzing statistics, we must take into consideration that a new house today cannot be compared with one that was built thirty years ago. The convenience, luxury and equipment that goes into the average American home today was something no one even dreamed about thirty years ago.

We repeat, America is not going down, but up. However, Europe is going up much faster! Actually, when we consider the market potential of Africa and Asia, specifically China, we begin to realize that the economic prosperity of the world is not coming to an end but is just beginning!

Military

As far as the military is concerned, we can summarize with these words: Politically speaking, the power of military might is being transferred from the "God Is Dead" power bloc (communism) to the "We Are Gods" power bloc (democracy).

Furthermore, the cry for a one world military force is being expressed more and more. An article in *The State,* dated December 3, 1993, asked the question:

EXPANSION OF NATO?
The United States proposed transforming the Cold War-era NATO alliance into a massive military and political partnership of as many as 40 nations to meet Europe's security needs. The initiative, which calls first for former Eastern adversaries of NATO to join peace-keeping operations and help draft defense budgets, was endorsed informally by foreign ministers of alliance members as "a huge step forward," Secretary General Manfred Woemer said. [33]

Fundamentally speaking, there is not much difference between NATO and the United Nations. Both have the same aim: Peace for the world at all cost.

United World Armed Forces

The U.N. is a force to be reckoned with. There is a sensible argument that goes like this: "You can't have two armies fighting each other when there is only one."

A one world army is not a theory existing only in the mind of some fiction writer, but it is becoming a workable reality today. The only hindrance for a world army at this moment is the United States military force. Nevertheless, the financial inferiority of Washington will sooner or later weaken the strong arm of the U.S..

Eventually, under the leadership of the Antichrist, the world will proudly and securely proclaim, *"Who is like unto the beast? who is able to make war with him?"* (Revelation 13:4). However, once again, the key to world dominion will not be achieved through weapons of war. It will be achieved through politics and economic necessity.

The Soviet Union, for example, was not defeated by a military force. They simply ran out of money. One may argue that Russia, not the U.S.A., is the hindrance to a world army.

That surely was the case before the collapse of the Soviet Union, but is no longer applicable because Russia has an even greater problem financially than the U.S.A.. They have learned that with party dictatorship, the people will not fully cooperate, thus, the resurrection of a power structure equal or superior to the West is out of the question. America's desperate hold on former glory is at this moment hindering the military unity of the world. Soon or later, this will have to change because the world must also become one militarily. A military superpower can only exist if it's matched by a super financial system!

How the Believer Should View These Events
How is the Church of Jesus Christ to view these developments? My answer is two words: "With joy!" Nowhere in the Bible do we find that Christians have a political, military or geographical promise. We are pilgrims just passing through.

The unity we see developing in the political, economic, military and religious world is just another great sign that we are going to be united with our Lord sooner than we may think. I am convinced that the words found in Luke 21:28 are applicable to us today: *"And when these things begin to come to pass, then look up, and lift up your heads; for your redemption draweth nigh."*

CHAPTER 11

The Arising of Global Unity

Summary

America's relationship to Rome reveals some astonishing facts. Eighty-seven percent of our immigrant forefathers came from Europe. While Europe was divided, America united. How Europe is changing today, and what it means to America, is highlighted in this chapter. We show how the arising global unity is being grounded upon a new world economy supported by the successful philosophy, "United we stand, divided we fall."

The Arising of Global Unity

I would like to emphasize again the four words of Revelation 17:13, *"...these have one mind...."* This is a great endtime miracle, namely, the almost perfect unity of people on Earth after the church is gone. This amazing unity, however, is nothing other than Satan's *imitation* of the Church of Jesus Christ.

Read the words of the High Priestly prayer of our Lord Jesus in John 17: In verse 22, He says, *"And the glory which thou gavest me I have given them; that they may be one, even as we are one."*

In verse 23 we read, *"I in them, and thou in me, that they may be made perfect in one; and that the world may know that thou hast sent me, and hast loved them, as thou hast loved me."* In order for Satan to deceive the nations of the world, he must produce that which looks like *"...they* (the world) *may be made perfect in one...."*

Unified Europe Imitates the Church

The Devil's actions in the kingdom of darkness through the spirit of the Antichrist are an imitation of the Spirit of God. We know that the Devil cannot create. He is the great imitator. He is the evil liar, the father of lies. He will attempt to imitate the unity possessed by the church, but it will only be a fraud.

Should we therefore be surprised to see Rome [Europe] aiming toward a goal of world dominion through a united effort? This dominance has no comparison to former dominions in history.

I repeat, we are already living within this new world order. In the past, one country conquered another, taking possession of territory and subjecting the citizens of the conquered country to the rulership of the conquerors.

This can also be said about the U.S.A.. Our forefathers came, conquered the land, destroyed all opposition by force of weapons, and established a new nation.

New World Order Rules

Today, the battles for new territory are no longer fought with weapons of war. The battle takes place in political offices and corporate boardrooms, as well as through the media. It is now virtually impossible to take over a country by military force.

For example, take Saddam Hussein's attempt to take over Kuwait. Virtually the entire world agreed to oppose Hussein's aggressive move and defeated him militarily. Why did the world oppose him? Because his action was a threat to the efforts being made toward a peaceful *new world order*.

Even assisting another nation without the popular support of the people has failed too, as was the case with America's war in Vietnam. Russia had a similar experience in Afghanistan. Shamefully defeated and embarrassed, they had to withdraw!

We are in a new world today. Different rules and regulations apply. After political unity is achieved, there won't be any need for diverse political opinions, or opposing parties. The people of the world will believe they have finally found the system that works to create a peaceful and prosperous worldwide society on Earth.

There will be no need for the overwhelming burden of keeping diverse governments, institutions, infrastructure in business, economy, commerce, industry, finance and military. God's Word says the people will *"...have one mind."*

Unity In Diversity

Hitler did not take over Germany by force; he was democratically elected. When he saw that the people really supported him with all of their hearts, minds, and souls, he then abolished all other political parties.

When the Antichrist comes to power, he is going to do likewise, and as a result, all people will virtually be one. This follows in line with the "politically correct" slogan today—"unity in diversity."

Someone may disagree and say that China, for example, is a communist country, contrary to capitalist democracy. That certainly is true, but that statement ignores the fact that China's economy is largely built on capitalist principles. They are creating a gigantic export market by using the social-capital system.

A modified form of communism has become a legitimate alternative in their political arena, meshing with the global democratic system that is now being built.

Four former East European countries have reelected communists into government. Over one-third of East Germany's citizens want communism back today. Yes, communism is being incorporated into the idea of "unity in diversity."

Global Corporations in the Lead
Multinational corporations are showing us the way. "Integrate," they say, "let one board of directors make decisions for multiple smaller firms." This is success, and you can't argue with success. Larger corporations are merging and buying out smaller ones continuously. We have multinational corporations which have become so powerful, they are now beginning to rule the economy, industry, financial institutions, and even the military in the countries where they operate.

We can't deny the fact that the military conflict with Iraq was economically motivated. Surely we can't believe that the United States and Canada, for example, went to the Gulf to liberate the poor oppressed Kuwaitis. If we believe that, we are likely to believe any fairy tale.

Global Corporate Identity
In an issue of the German language *Focus* magazine, an article reported that the board of directors of Mercedes Benz were challenged by some experts to consider changing its standard procedure of imprinting their products with the label "Made in Germany." It was argued that many products are now being

made in different countries. The proposal was made to replace the "Made in Germany" label with "Made by Mercedes." While this has not happened yet, we see the possibility in the near future.

Most international corporations like Mercedes Benz have manufacturing or assembling facilities in dozens of countries around the world. Hence, we are seeing a new trend taking place as multinationals expand and become more powerful.

Employees are now being identified with the company they work for to such an extent that they are becoming fully integrated with the name of the company. For example, John Doe, who works for General Motors in Detroit, Michigan would simply be identified as "John Doe of General Motors." Thus, unity based on citizenship will decrease and give room to unity through an alliance of global corporations.

20th Century Success Story

The greatest success story of a nation in this century is no doubt the story of the United States of America. We have already spoken about the conflict Europe has been involved in for so many centuries. The discovery of America opened two important avenues for the development of endtime events.

- The energy of Europeans had to be expanded and the vast open spaces of the Americas offered the perfect opportunity for them.

- For the first time since the Roman world empire, Europeans had to work together in spite of diverse culture, language, heritage, and mentality. North America, with a climate similar to Europe, offered the greatest opportunity.

What occurred during these short 200 years, specifically the last 100, is now history. The experiment to have Europeans work together, live together, and unite under one nationality turned out to be a smashing success.

It is no surprise, therefore, that many important global organizations, such as the United Nations, were founded here in the U.S..

If Europeans from so many different nations, including Africans and Asians, came together and formed a successful nation, then why would this not be applicable to Europe?

But there is more. This system of unity created out of diversity could also be applied to the entire world.

Not only was the United States extremely successful in industry, agriculture, politics, and religion, but the result of creating a new identity from among the diverse people of the world is even more astonishing.

Mixture of the Nation's Success

I am well aware that my analysis of the United States is somewhat prejudiced. I am not residing in some foreign country far away from the U.S., trying to analyze the nation and the people, but I have been a part of it for the last 32 years. This has become my country.

The greatest thing that can happen to anyone happened to me in the U.S.. I found the Lord Jesus in this country, or better, He found me. I found my wife, Ruth, in America and my three sons, Joel, Micah and Simon, were born here. Not only are they Americans on paper as I am, but they think, act, and exhibit Americanism.

From all of my travels in the world and my association with diverse people, I have never found a more upright, polite, and generous people than Americans.

I am also convinced that there are innumerable people from around the world who come to the same conclusion. Therefore, the questions arise, "Why not have a one world society?

What's wrong with the new world order wherein all people can move freely to any country they desire? Why can't we be a one world family?"

These questions, dear friends, are very natural and legitimate. It is for these and many other reasons that I have no time nor energy to oppose these ideas. This is fulfillment of Bible prophecy. It tells me that the world is becoming one. Subsequently, Jesus must be coming soon, and therefore, I shall invest all of my time, energy, and finances in proclaiming the liberating Gospel of the Lord Jesus Christ to all people everywhere.

Success Story: U.S.A.
Let me reinforce the success story of the United States of America. The approximately 38 million newcomers to the U.S.A. from 1820 and 1940, included the following major groups of peoples:

6.0 million Germans	4.7 million Italians
4.5 million Irish	4.2 million British
3.5 million Russians (from the former Soviet Union)	
2.5 million Austrians	1.5 million Swedish

However, they all became one: One nation, with one language, one currency, government, military and economy, under one flag!

While the U.S.A. began to prosper around the late 1800's, and no longer was considered a poverty-stricken, primitive, uncultured new land, Europe was in turmoil. The United States had not only become a nation to be reckoned with, but in the process, superseded all other nations in the world including Europe. The U.S. became the undisputed global leader at the beginning of 1900 and held the lead for about 70 years. What has happened thereafter? Let me explain.

The Change of Guard

While many of us, specifically in the field of prophetic teaching, desperately seek an answer as to why Europe has superseded the U.S., I propose that we look at this development as a simple fulfillment of Bible prophecy.

How can the United States become subject unto Europe if it is more powerful? How can Europe become the power center of the world if it has not outdistanced all nations including the U.S.A.?

The logical answer to these two questions are sufficient to prove beyond a shadow of doubt that we are now approaching the last stages of the endtime which will establish world rulership through the social-capital democratic system.

Which Land of Opportunity?

America is still a land of great opportunity, but not for all people, specifically those who are well-educated and talented. We refer to an article in *The State*, July 6th, 1995, on page B10:

> The United States is the land of opportunity for fewer and fewer foreigners whose special skills give them the right to immigrate here, U.S. officials say.
>
> Newly released Justice Department statistics show that highly educated professionals from other countries are spurning the chance to apply for U.S. citizenship under immigration preferences for workers in key fields.
>
> In the last fiscal year, the number of immigrants legally admitted to this country for employment reasons plunged by 16 percent, mostly because eligible professionals failed to apply, officials said.
>
> Since 1993, the number of immigrant visas granted to scientists, academics, managers and others with special training declined to 123,291 from 147,012, the Justice Department reported, blaming the shortfall on a dearth of applicants.

"There were fewer takers," said Greg Gagne, spokesman for the Immigration and Naturalization Service.

Labor experts said the drop in applications from professionals appears to reflect a decline in the number of high-wage jobs in the U.S. economy, even as demand for low-wage workers remains high. [34]

The new immigration statistics reveal prophetic tendencies. The success of the United States as a nation was mainly due to the mixing of nationalities. Almost 37 million came from Europe, the overwhelming majority of them in search of a better life.

The key to success was unity as we have already seen. Therefore, the logical question follows: "If people of different nationalities could be integrated successfully into one, creating a new nation, why can't the Europeans become united on their own continent?"

That is why Europe is in the process of becoming one, and therefore, the center of success is shifting back to Europe.

The July, 1994 issue of *Money* magazine reported that 250,000 Americans were leaving the U.S.A. for good, in search of better opportunities elsewhere.

In order for Bible prophecy to be fulfilled, Rome (Europe) must rule the world. Nations who would challenge Europe, like the U.S., must decrease in their importance. This trend is already taking place today. Never could Europe challenge America on its own merits while it remained divided into individual sovereign nations. But a united Europe would be able to challenge anyone. The idea of becoming of "one mind" like the U.S., began to take root.

United Europe Under Rome

It is important to emphasize that the dream of a united Europe is not new. It was a reality under the Roman world empire.

No European nation can write her history without mentioning Rome. Rome with its culture, glory, philosophy and politics defined Europe's civilization. In fact, there was a certain degree of liberation for the people during the Roman era. I will prove this from the Bible in just a moment.

The great philosophers and statesmen throughout history always spoke about the unity of the Roman empire, this power bloc that could not be challenged by any nation of the world!

"How did Rome become so powerful?" we may ask. The answer can be given in one word: "unity." When Rome conquered Europe, the Mediterranean nations, and parts of Asia and Northern Africa, she did not enslave the people, as is often claimed, but rather gave them liberty. Our thinking has been influenced strongly by Hollywood movies which show Roman soldiers whipping people into submission. That was true only as an exception.

Even to the middle of the 1900's, whipping offenders was the law in many countries, among which was Britain. For example, Jews that were caught in Palestine opposing the military occupation of that land by Britain were frequently whipped!

Roman Citizenship: The Desire of Europe
Oppressed people never accomplish anything. The glorious empire which Rome built was due to the fact that the people wanted to be part of this success story, and served Caesar with all of their heart. They were extremely proud to be called Romans. They virtually surrendered themselves to the jurisdiction of Rome and welcomed the new liberty that was guaranteed by Caesar.

The Hitler Connection
It was like this during Hitler's time as well. The people literally worshiped Adolf Hitler in Germany, Austria and in many

other countries. They wanted this man to rule by all means. They even prayed for him because they thought he was a man God sent for salvation and redemption, peace and prosperity. They were deceived, of course, just as people are being deceived today by the success of democracy.

Rome conquered nation after nation, not only by military power, but by the promise of integration, offering them Roman citizenship, protection and prosperity. They had a chance to become Romans, to be integrated into the world's greatest society.

Provision was made for the new citizen to retain and practice his own religion. The philosophy—that there are many gods—was tolerated, but only under the name of Caesar.

"I Was Born Free," Paul States

The significance of Roman citizenship is amplified for us in the Scripture. In Acts 22 we see the event that deals with the Apostle Paul. In verses 25–29, we read: *"And as they bound him with thongs, Paul said unto the centurion that stood by, Is it lawful for you to scourge a man that is a Roman, and uncondemned? When the centurion heard that, he went and told the chief captain, saying, Take heed what thou doest: for this man is a Roman.*

"Then the chief captain came, and said unto him, Tell me, art thou a Roman? He said, Yea. And the chief captain answered, With a great sum obtained I this freedom. And Paul said, But I was free born.

"Then straightway they departed from him which should have examined him: and the chief captain also was afraid, after he knew that he was a Roman, and because he had bound him."

Now, that's a powerful statement. Paul was born under Roman rule. He was a Roman, he had inherited his citizenship by birth. Freedom and liberty were guaranteed to him. This is plainly evident from the chief captain who apparently was a naturalized citizen, and not Roman by birth.

There was a great cost involved in becoming a Roman citizen, *"...The chief captain answered, With a great sum obtained I this freedom...."* To that, Paul simply replied, *"...but I was free born...."* He was born a Roman citizen.

U.S.A. In Roman Footsteps

The United States followed in the footsteps of the Roman system. Automatic citizenship is granted to any person born in the U.S.A.. Those not born in America must go through the process of naturalization if they wish to become citizens.

Most of us do not realize the fact that our immigrant forefathers paid a tremendous price to become Americans. Think of those who came before the 1800's up to the early 1900's. Not only did it cost them a lot of money for the fare, (that was the least of their worries), but when they left Europe, it was, for most, goodbye forever! Never would they have a chance to return to their homeland. They went from the highly cultured, well-organized and affluent Europe, to a faraway land of wilderness, poverty, lawlessness, and sickness, and all of these challenges were faced without extended family. They surrendered their heritage, their language, and most of all, suffered the loss of their national identity. That indeed is a great price to pay! However, and this is most significant, the loss of virtually everything by our forefathers was for the purpose of gaining something that was hoped for: more individual freedom, land ownership, and ultimate prosperity. Unfortunately, this was rarely the case for the immigrants. Most often it only became true for their descendants.

A New Way For the New World

Our immigrant forefathers started something totally new without any guarantees of success.

They must have been courageous people who had faith in a new existence. Many had faith in the living God. Burning the bridges to the old continent gave our forefathers a creative spirit to do things different, which later became known as "the American way!"

Unlike most other colonial lands, which were fed intellectually, philosophically, financially and militarily by their mother country in Europe, American forefathers cut many ties, including traditional religion.

Faith in God

Faith in the living God became more important than faith in the traditional European religion.

Many Americans took the Bible as the Word of God point blank. They preached the Gospel of salvation in simplicity to whoever had an ear to hear. The result was astonishing. Hundreds of thousands were converted to living faith in the Lord Jesus Christ. America became the undisputed capital of the Gospel of Jesus Christ for the entire world!

Even to this day, America is responsible for most of the world's missionary activity. No doubt, therefore, much of the success of the United States can also be found in its citizens' simple faith in the living God of the Bible.

Foreign Aid

It is no wonder, then, that America, contrary to virtually all other nations, practiced compassion, even upon her enemies. The blood of the last American soldier killed in action in Germany was not even cold when Americans started loading ships with food to feed the conquered Germans.

During that time, no other nation on the face of the Earth gave as much in foreign aid as did America. It was a time when the U.S. was the undisputed leader in the living standards of the world.

It is striking that during the last several decades, the population of America has protested against giving foreign aid. And the voices of protest are becoming louder today.

Even more astonishing is the fact that the right wing, overwhelmingly supported by Bible-believing Christians, now vehemently opposes foreign aid! We have to wonder if this has any relationship to the fact that America today is number eighteen in supplying foreign aid to other countries. Not less surprising, therefore, is the fact that American's standard of living is down to number eight from number one!

Religious Freedom

Freedom of religion for the sake of political union, which was guaranteed in the Constitution equally for Jews, Catholics, and others, was another milestone in the remarkable U.S. success story.

Even though the Catholic church had severely persecuted Protestants in Europe, they were allowed to prosper here mostly unhindered. With the tolerance of religion, however, the occult found a fertile ground here, too.

Our first President, George Washington, and many of the founding fathers, were members of the occult religion of Freemasonry. Mormons, Jehovah Witnesses, Christian Scientists, and multiple other cults are a product of religious freedom. But the new nationality brought forth by the immigrants overbridged the religious diversity.

In Europe, not only nationality, but specifically, religion was the major hindering element for unity. Today, however, the story has changed dramatically. Religion has become insignificant throughout Europe.

Tolerance is at an all-time high because the bulk of the population does not take religion seriously. The dismal state of religious attachment has opened the door for Europeans to unite.

To conclude this chapter, I would like to make an important point. We who are born again of the Spirit of God are eternal heavenly citizens. Our home is in heaven, whether we live in the United States, Canada, Mexico, Germany, France, Italy, England, or any other country. It makes no difference. We are just passing through. Our position is eternally settled in heaven. We are perfectly one in the Lord Jesus Christ!

Are you born again? If not, you belong to a political identity of a nation. You have no hope, no future, and no eternal life in our Lord.

CHAPTER 12

Europe Beyond 2000

Summary

The coming European power-house will produce the system that creates the "ten king" empire. We review Europe's development from 1957 to the present.

Not capitalism, or communism, but *social-capital democracy* is becoming the driving force of the union which will supersede all others. A new world order is in the infancy today, but it will become the deceiving philosophy beyond the year 2000.

Europe Beyond 2000
How has Europe progressed since the Treaty of Rome was
signed in 1957, the beginning of the new Europe?

The Original Six in 1957
Six countries were the original signatories to the Roman treaty:

Belgium . . . . . .10.0 million	*France* . . . . . .57.2 million
Germany . . . . .80.2 million	*Italy* . . . . .57.8 million
Luxembourg . . . .0.4 million	*Netherlands* . .15.1 million

Thus, a total of 220.7 million people became part of a cooper-
ative effort to create a new Europe. After the initial success of
establishing the common market, other European countries
recognized the promising future of this new movement.
A number of nations applied for membership.

Three More Nations in 1973
In January of 1973, three more nations were accepted:

Denmark . . . . . .5.2 million	*Ireland* . . . . . . 3.5 million
Britain . . . . . . .57.6 million	

Thus another 66.3 million were added! Now united Europe had
overtaken the United States in population.

Greece Makes Number 10
After 1973, there was an eight-year lull. Then in 1981, Greece
was added to the European Economic Community. This step
was rather unusual. Although Greece belongs to Europe, it is
more identifiable in association with Mediterranean countries
and was expected to be one of the last to be accepted.

Greece . . . . . . .10.3 million

When Greece came into the fold of the European Economic Community, the new Europe counted 297 million citizens.

I believe there is a specific reason for having Greece added to Europe in 1981. Earlier, I mentioned that according to the Bible, Greece constituted the third gentile world empire.

We also saw how the gentile empires were enumerated: Babylon, Medo-Persia, Greece, and Rome, symbolized by four metals—gold, silver, brass, and iron.

Further, we saw that these four empires are identifiable in our day and all four were involved in war in recent decades. The enumeration of these power structures is significant, *"Then was the iron, the clay, the brass, the silver, and the gold, broken to pieces together..."* (Daniel 2:35a). The head, which is Babylon, is not going to be broken first, but the feet, the softest part, the most inferior system. When Daniel interprets the dream, he cautions, *"...it brake in pieces the iron, the brass, the clay, the silver, and the gold..."* (Daniel 2:45). The iron is Rome [European Union] and the brass is Greece.

Therefore, we can expect that Iran [Persia], the silver empire, will one day be added as well. Finally, Iraq, which was ancient Babylon, the gold empire, must be incorporated in the European Union (Roman empire) as well.

While these conclusions are not clearly visible yet, we know from the Holy Scripture that these empires will become united because they must stand in the final judgment.

1986: Europe 336.4 Million Strong
The development of the European Union continued. In 1986, Portugal and Spain were also accepted.

Portugal . . . . . . .9.9 million   *Spain* . . . . . . .40.0 million

The EEC in 1986 was thus 336.4 million strong! Less than 30 years after the birth of the Treaty of Rome in 1957, Europe had become the most powerful economic bloc in the world. Since 1994, she has been known as the European Union.

Who Are the Ten Kings?

It has commonly been believed by many Bible scholars that the European Union was a fulfillment of the resurrected Roman empire. It was also commonly believed that the E.U. would only have ten nations. But as we have just seen, when Spain and Portugal were added, the number rose to twelve.

The conclusion that the E.U. would be made up of ten nations originated with the misinterpretation of Revelation 17:12, where it speaks of ten kings.

A Voice From 1967

Midnight Call founder, Dr. Wim Malgo, wrote in 1967:

> Let us not look for ten countries being members of the European Common Market constituting the fulfillment of Revelation 17:12. Rather we must look for ten power structures that will develop through the European initiative but will be worldwide.

I have always been in full agreement with this statement because the Bible specifically says ten "kings." A king is not a nation. He is an individual person. While it is too early to properly identify who these ten power structures are, there is no doubt that Europe will be number one. This is not only because it has the most educated population, the biggest economic power bloc, and innumerable other advantages, but because Europe is the foundation of our modern civilization and is willing to change.

History shows that whenever a group of peoples or a nation was willing to change, such as was the case with America, it reinvented itself in a new process of creative thinking.

Social-Capital Democracy

Today, America dreams of "Old Glory" while Europe is looking toward a new unknown future. There is no doubt in my mind that the one who takes the risk is the winner.

One thing is relatively sure: From the presently functioning democratic systems, none will emerge as the clear winner in Europe. Thus, compromise is the key to the success of merging the various political thinking patterns into one.

Because Europe has strong socialist tendencies and plans to accept former communist countries as members, I venture to say that a new system will be created that I would like to describe as a "social capital democratic system."

We already mentioned that China would fiercely oppose American capitalist democracy.

Yet, a social-capital system is acceptable.

What is Socialism?

During the time of the existence of the Soviet Union, communism was outrightly rejected by progressive Western nations. Socialism, too, was rejected by the United States specifically, but accepted in Europe. Because socialism was considered the precursor of communism, the United States abhorred the thought of it. However, when we investigate the meaning of socialism, we quickly find that without it, no nation could, in reality, exist.

During one of our prophecy conferences, I asked the audience, "How many socialists do we have present today?" I saw not one hand raised. I rephrased my question and asked, "How many do not have at least one insurance policy?" Two or three lifted their hands and I assume they did not quite understand my question. Then I made the following statement: "You have bought an insurance policy to protect yourself in case of an accident or a catastrophe, so someone else will pay your bill. That is socialism!"

Do We Really OWN Property?

Another example: My son Micah casually asked me the question at the beginning of the year, "Have you paid your lease on your house, Papa?"

I answered, "I don't lease the house. I own it. I paid for it."

Then he countered, "Try not to pay your lease to your local tax office and the government will take your house and lease it to someone else."

How true that statement was! A form of socialism is present in all societies, and without it, it could not function. To be social is a form of socialism. You must be sensitive to the wishes of your neighborhood. You simply can not do as you please under the pretense that you are living in a free country.

Let's say you do not wish to participate in the social services available in your neighborhood. You want to be independent. Cut off electricity, telephone, water, sewerage, gas, and all other public amenities.

Then, begin to dig your own well for water, install your own septic tank in accordance with your free independent spirit and start cooking on a wood-burning stove or even on an outside fire. It would not take very long for the neighbors to complain to the authorities and rightly so.

The accumulation of trash, and the constant smoke of your fire, would certainly be an unpleasant sight and smell to the neighbors, and the authorities would force you to conform socially.

Even in finances and industry, socialism is at work in the United States. Remember when the United States government had to bail out Chrysler Corporation from financial disaster? Today, they are a healthy prospering industrial giant. That, too, is socialism.

What about our farmers? Here too, we see socialism in action. The government guarantees income—with immense subsidies—for the continuous existence of farmers who cannot compete successfully in the global market with their products. That is not free capitalistic enterprise, it is socialism.

Especially when it works, you will not hear any protests against socialism. Today, not only in the United States, but in virtually all countries in the world, except a few African nations, farmers are producing such an abundance that quite frequently, products have to be destroyed in order to stabilize prices and avoid financial ruin.

This type of socialism has always been accepted in Europe and their experience in that field is now helping Europe to prosper even more.

Europe: Fifteen Nations
On January 1st, 1995, three more nations joined the Union:

Austria . . . . .8.0 million   *Sweden* . . . . . .8.6 million
Finland . . . . . . .5.0 million

At the time of this writing, the E.U. is over 362 million strong. And there are more nations, especially from Eastern Europe, that are waiting to join. Therefore, we must emphasize that it appears the E.U. will continue to grow in size and number. It will, I believe, eventually expand across the globe comprising ten power structures.

Most important, however, is to understand that no other group of nations can claim to be the center of the world's intellect except Europe. They are the originators of our global westernized civilization. No doubt, Europe is being readied for world dominion!

United Economy
Daniel prophesied of this last kingdom some 2,500 years ago, *"Thus he said, The fourth beast shall be the fourth kingdom upon earth, which shall be diverse from all kingdoms, and*

shall devour the whole earth, and shall tread it down, and break it in pieces" (Daniel 7:23). Notice Daniel says the last kingdom will devour *"...the whole earth...."*

The phenomenal growth of Europe is based strictly on economy and finance at this point in time. The economy is virtually united already. Although Europe does not have a unified currency right now, they are well on the road to establishing one. The following was published in *The European*, July 6, 1995, on p.17:

Currency Target: 1999

The Cannes summit recognized that 1999 is a more realistic date than January 1, 1997, for the beginning of the final stage of monetary union, due to culminate in the changeover to a single currency. As set out by the European Commission's May, 1995 green paper, the three main steps of the final phase will be spread out over about four years.

• Late 1997: The E.U. Council decides which countries meet the convergence criteria.

• January, 1998: Dates for the start of the final stage and for the introduction of the single currency are announced; the European Monetary Institute prepares to become a fully fledged central bank. Preparations for the switch to a single currency, including those for all legal contracts (such as mortgages), intensify.

• January 1999 (at the latest): Exchange rates are irrevocably fixed between participating countries; the European central bank (ECB) takes over; the ECU becomes a common currency in which monetary policy operations are conducted; governments issue debt in the single currency; financial markets and the private sector switch to the single currency; retail transactions are still made in national currencies.

• January 2002 (at the latest): All transactions in the participating countries must be denominated in the single currency. In a matter of weeks, coins and bank notes denominated in the single currency must be substituted for the "old" means of payment. Those countries not ready for monetary union must continue their efforts to meet the criteria and their currencies will remain within the exchange rate mechanism of the European monetary system.[35]

Global Currency

While there is much doubt and uncertainty about the E.U. finally coming to terms with the requirements for the new currency called "euro," it doesn't take much imagination to see the reality of a European currency when considering how Europe looked just 50 years ago. With the coming new European currency, we will likely see in the not-too-distant future that the price of oil will be paid in Euro currency.

Already, the Organization of Petroleum Exporting Countries (OPEC) is lamenting the continuous fall of the U.S. dollar. Many voices are being heard in favor of replacing the U.S. dollar as the world's dominant currency.

Actually, a world currency is already here in practical terms. For example, when you take your credit card and travel to any part of the world, you can instantaneously buy virtually anything in any currency. If you have a U.S. credit card, you will be billed in your own currency back home, and the shop keeper, restaurant or hotel will be paid in their local currency. We don't have to wait for a one world financial system to appear because it is already working right now at this moment! The world already functions as a global economic community.

Religion

This last gentile empire will be strongly saturated with occultism. As a matter of fact, a devilish religion will be essential to the success of the economic system. The words of the prophet Daniel read: *"And in the latter time of their kingdom, when the transgressors are come to the full, a king of fierce countenance, and understanding dark sentences, shall stand up"* (Daniel 8:23). Obviously, the phrase, *"...understanding dark sentences..."* reveals this king's deep involvement in the occult. Verse 24 continues, *"And his power shall be mighty, but not by his own power: and he shall destroy wonderfully, and shall prosper, and practise, and shall destroy the mighty and the holy people."* It is of extreme significance that his power is *"...not by his own power...."*

The identity of this king is given in detail in Revelation 13. When you read the first 8 verses of this chapter, you will see repeatedly that this *first* beast, the Antichrist, has no power of his own. Verse 2 reads, *"...and the dragon gave him his power, and his seat, and great authority."* Verse 4, *"And they worshipped the dragon which gave power unto the beast: and they worshipped the beast, saying, Who is like unto the beast? who is able to make war with him?"* This Scripture clearly identifies that he will also be the supreme military ruler.

Then, verse 5: *"And there was given unto him a mouth speaking great things and blasphemies; and power was given unto him to continue forty and two months."* Verse 7 says, *"And it was given unto him to make war with the saints, and to overcome them: and power was given him over all kindreds, and tongues, and nations."* Repeatedly, we see that the Antichrist receives power *directly* from the great dragon, Satan.

Antichrist and Europe

Based on the Scripture that the Antichrist has no power on his own merits, he probably is an insignificant person who will receive the needed support, prestige, and power directly from Satan. It is therefore an error to seek out a certain important, powerful personality in our time and try to identify him as the coming Antichrist.

Although the Bible doesn't tell us plainly who the Antichrist will be, it does give characteristics of what he will be like. For example, in Daniel 8:24 we read: *"...he shall destroy wonderfully...."* This is the elimination of all other systems which we have had previously or will have at that time. We know that Nazism has failed, and that communism will never attain its former glory. The present form of capitalism will also be replaced with the new social-capital system which is already prospering in Europe.

Success By Deception
Let us read this verse from the Hebrew Bible:

> By his cunning, he will use deceit successfully. He will make great plans, will destroy many, taking them unawares, and will rise up against the chief of Chiefs, but will be broken, not by [human] hands.

I must add here that the success of the Antichrist and his new world system, headquartered in Europe, is not only due to his deceptive work, but it is permitted by God. God is in absolute control. Even though Satan rules this world, God is still on the throne.

Before I explain my statement, let me read from Amos 3:6, *"...shall there be evil in a city, and the LORD hath not done it?"* This means that God knows every evil intention of Satan, and He will permit it to come to pass, according to His counsel. The deception that is going to be so successful is also due to the fact that God gives people up who continuously refuse to listen to the truth, who reject the love which He has offered now for almost 2000 years.

Thus, in 2nd Thessalonians 2:11 we read: *"And for this cause God shall send them strong delusion, that they should believe a lie."*

What a joy it is to read the last sentence of that verse in Daniel 8:25, *"...but he* [Antichrist] *shall be broken without hand."*

When Jesus comes in great power and glory, He does not need to confront the evil one in a desperate battle. Satan was defeated when Jesus cried out on Calvary's cross, *"...It is finished!"* But when Jesus comes back to Earth to set up His millennial kingdom, Satan's visible power is broken, too: *"... then shall that Wicked be revealed, whom the Lord shall consume with the spirit of his mouth, and shall destroy with the brightness of his coming"* (2nd Thessalonians 2:8).

Focus on Europe
The success of Europe today, and its even greater success in the future, point out in unmistakably clear terms that God is permitting the reestablishment of the old Roman empire.

The spirit of Antichrist, which proclaims freedom, justice, liberty, and prosperity for all people through democracy, is being supported wholeheartedly by the majority of the world's population.

Today, it is virtually impossible for any nation to reject democracy. Thus, we must focus our eyes even more on Europe and the Middle East. This is where it all began and this is where it will end. Rome ruled when Jesus was born and Rome will rule when Jesus comes again!

Our Hope
Finally, I must emphasize, we who believe in the Lord Jesus Christ are not integrated into this system. We are *in* the world, but not *of* the world. We are not placing our hope in a better United States, a higher standard of living, or the implementation of justice and righteousness.

Our home is with the Eternal One, where we will meet Jesus! We have no promise nor command to solve the political problems of this world. No matter how hard we try, we will never eliminate crime, pornography, homosexuality, corruption, and the horrible murder of the unborn.

We are unable to impose justice and liberty for this world, because the world is unwilling to bend the knee to Jesus Christ. One thing, however, we must do, according to the Bible: *"But ye, brethren, are not in darkness, that that day should overtake you as a thief. Ye are all the children of light, and the children of the day: we are not of the night, nor of darkness.*

"Therefore let us not sleep, as do others; but let us watch and be sober" (1st Thessalonians 5:4–6).

As believers, we must understand that God rules the entire universe, but He permits Satan, the great imitator, the father of lies, to do his work of deception. Thus, the world today is full of hope that they, by themselves, based on their own intellect, will bring about peace which they never have experienced before.

The real peace, we know from the prophetic Word, is when Jesus comes to establish His kingdom in Israel and rule the world with a rod of iron. The nations will become subject unconditionally to the Lord. That is the only true and lasting peace that will come about. Thus, the Devil is now desperately working on bringing about a peace that is strictly based on the achievement of human beings. The most successful tool for this is democracy.

CHAPTER 13

The Fake and the Final Kingdom

Summary

In order for the last gentile world empire to be replaced by God's Kingdom, we must realize that first, the fake kingdom (gentile) must be fully established. In that process, the distinction between Jews and gentiles will be erased. The temple in Jerusalem will be rebuilt and animal sacrifice will be reinstituted. Then, the hidden conflict will become apparent with the Antichrist opposing Israel.

The Final and the Fake Kingdom

Let us read in Daniel 2:44, *"And in the days of these kings shall the God of heaven set up a kingdom, which shall never be destroyed: and the kingdom shall not be left to other people, but it shall break in pieces and consume all these kingdoms, and it shall stand for ever."*

Please note that the kingdom spoken of here, *"...which shall never be destroyed..."* is the kingdom of Israel. In spite of the fact that Israel was nonexistent for over 2,000 years, particularly with the destruction of the temple in A.D. 70, from God's point of view, this kingdom never ceased to exist.

God confirms the unconditional covenant He had made with David to his son Solomon. In 1st Kings 9:5 we read, *"... I will establish the throne of thy kingdom upon Israel for ever, as I promised to David thy father, saying, There shall not fail thee a man upon the throne of Israel."* Yet, for 2,000 years, we did not see Israel as a visible reality. It simply did not exist in the visible world.

Zechariah, the father of John the Baptist, received the words, *"...He* [Jesus] *shall reign over the house of Jacob for ever; and of his kingdom there shall be no end"* (Luke 1:33). Just to make sure that this is eternal (never ending), let's read what Daniel says, *"But the saints of the most High shall take the kingdom, and possess the kingdom for ever, even for ever and ever"* (Daniel 7:18).

In the last days it will be the kingdom through which the entire four gentile empires will be destroyed, *"Forasmuch as thou sawest that the stone was cut out of the mountain without hands, and that it brake in pieces the iron, the brass, the clay, the silver, and the gold; the great God hath made known to the king what shall come to pass hereafter: and the dream is certain, and the interpretation thereof sure"* (Daniel 2:45).

This verse simply describes the end of the entire gentile world in just a few words!

Daniel Sees Europe

I don't think we need to explain further that all systems, whether dictatorship, monarchy, socialism, Nazism, communism, or democracy, will be destroyed and replaced with the kingdom of God which will be established by the Lord Jesus Christ.

We have just read the confirmation in Daniel 2. What is the Scriptural basis for the belief that God will establish His kingdom on Earth? Please remember that the Lord's first message was, *"...Repent ye: for the kingdom of heaven is at hand."* Israel, however, rejected the Messiah, thus, they rejected the kingdom. But that does not void God's eternal resolutions. The kingdom *will* be established!

Let's identify the time period when some of these things were fulfilled and when we can expect the final fulfillment.

The Coming Prince

Daniel gives us the answer in chapter 9, verses 25–27, *"Know therefore and understand, that from the going forth of the commandment to restore and to build Jerusalem unto the Messiah the Prince shall be seven weeks, and threescore and two weeks: the street shall be built again, and the wall, even in troublous times. And after threescore and two weeks shall Messiah be cut off, but not for himself: and the people of the prince that shall come shall destroy the city and the sanctuary; and the end thereof shall be with a flood, and unto the end of the war desolations are determined.*

"And he shall confirm the covenant with many for one week: and in the midst of the week he shall cause the sacrifice and the oblation to cease, and for the overspreading of abominations he shall make it desolate, even until the consummation, and that determined shall be poured upon the desolate."

This occurred when the Jews rebuilt the temple in Jerusalem, after they returned from the Babylonian captivity.

"And after threescore and two weeks shall Messiah be cut off, but not for himself...." The Messiah, Jesus Christ, died on the cross during the time of the Roman occupation of Israel and Jerusalem. Thus, we clearly have the identity of the empire of Jesus' time.

Who destroyed the city and the sanctuary? *"...And the people of the prince that shall come shall destroy the city and the sanctuary...."* It is a historical fact that Rome destroyed the "sanctuary" which can also be proven archaeologically. The city of Jerusalem and the temple were destroyed by the Roman army under Titus in A.D. 70.

Now, who is the prince that is referred to in the previous verse? Let's continue to read, *"...and the end thereof shall be with a flood, and unto the end of the war desolations are determined. And he shall confirm the covenant with many for one week: and in the midst of the week he shall cause the sacrifice and the oblation to cease, and for the overspreading of abominations he shall make it desolate, even until the consummation, and that determined shall be poured upon the desolate."* So, the prince is the Antichrist who will confirm a covenant with Israel. We need to recognize that the above verses deal with four time periods.

- The *first* starts with the return of the Jewish captives to Jerusalem to rebuild the temple.
- The *second* period is the renovation of the temple by King Herod under Roman jurisdiction.
- The *third* period begins with the destruction of that temple in A.D. 70 by Rome.
- The *fourth* period will be during the third rebuilding of the temple. That is yet to come. Animal sacrifice will be instituted, but will cease because the prince, the Antichrist, will cause it to cease. This has not happened yet.

Great Tribulation: Not Yet

There is an interpretation that says these things were fulfilled when the second temple was destroyed by the Romans in A.D. 70. This is incorrect. When Jesus refers to Daniel's prophecy, *"...when ye shall see the abomination of desolation, spoken of by Daniel the prophet..."* He reveals that the existence of a new temple and the sacrificial service must be reinstituted. That has not taken place yet.

Jesus describes the time of the Great Tribulation for us in Matthew 24:21: *"For then shall be great tribulation, such as was not since the beginning of the world to this time, no, nor ever shall be."* Thereby, we know that the Great Tribulation has not taken place yet, nor can we accept the interpretation that the Great Tribulation took place in A.D. 70 when the Romans destroyed Jerusalem and the sanctuary.

Sacrifice Reinstituted

Now we come to an important question. Why will the Antichrist *"...cause the sacrifice and the oblation to cease..."*? One theory I present is that the Antichrist could come under severe pressure from the world's religious and animal protection agencies which are active globally, expressing their displeasure at this apparent brutal slaughter of innocent animals.

Let me explain. The assumption that the Antichrist will be an oppressive dictator is fundamentally wrong. He will rule the most sophisticated, civilized, and well-educated democratic society in all of history.

Daniel says he will come peaceably and he will *"...obtain the kingdom by flatteries."* Just as today, no leader of the world will be elected to a political office unless he comes *peaceably*, and presents his case with *flatteries*, making promises which usually are lies. The people will gladly support his policies. They will promote his economic and judicial system. They will even accept the mark of the beast gladly. We must not overlook the fact that the entire world will worship the Antichrist, *"...all that dwell upon the earth shall worship him...."* You can only worship *voluntarily.*

The Antichrist, being a political genius, will probably have to carefully monitor the people of the world, just as the president of the United States monitors the citizens and tries to please them as much as he can, because he wants to be reelected.

Animal Sacrifices Abolished

During the Tribulation, Israel will rebuild the temple and will practice animal sacrifice, something that is contrary to the sensitivities of the entire world, even today. To assume that animal rights groups will have no voice during the Tribulation seems to be denying political reality. Therefore, I am absolutely convinced that the Antichrist will be influenced strongly by the people. His decision to cease the sacrifice takes place at the zenith of his success. There is no major religious faith in today's world that practices animal sacrificing in their worship. When the Jews do it, it will certainly set them apart. No doubt, the Antichrist will have the backing of the world for the abolishment of such a practice.

Self-Esteem and Self-Image Worshiped

Having appeased animal rights activists, he will then present himself as a substitute.

However, he will not become the sacrifice himself. Rather, in accordance with the then-prevailing world religion, fully established by the false teaching that man is God, the Antichrist will proclaim *himself* to be God. Thus we read in 2nd Thessalonians 2:4 that the Antichrist *"...opposeth and exalteth himself above all that is called God, or that is worshipped; so that he as God sitteth in the temple of God, shewing himself that he is God."*

Now, someone may think that my idea is far-fetched. Surely people will not believe and accept the proclamation of a man being God. If you believe this, just check your local bookstore and seek out the religious section where you will find an abundance of books for sale which clearly teach that man himself is god. To religions such as Hinduism, it is not such a strange idea. In general, the bulk of the world's religions accept the theory that man has a "god nature" within him, and therefore, in due time, he may progress to godhood.

To reinforce my statement that man is readily willing to accept a man-god, let me quote two pages from Dr. Dave Breese's book, *Know The Marks of Cults*:

In 1954, Sun Myung Moon founded the "Holy Spirit Association for the Unification of World Christianity." This Korean millionaire religious promoter claims hundreds of thousands of followers worldwide and fosters in them the belief that he is the "Lord of the Second Advent," the personalized second coming of Jesus Christ. Moon rose out of his Presbyterian and Pentecostal background to organize a cult around a new theology that presents him as the great hope for mankind. He and his second wife are put forth as the new Adam and Eve, and their followers are the first children of a new and perfect world.

Judge Rutherford of the Jehovah's Witnesses presented himself as "God's chosen vessel" and the Watchtower organization as the final dispenser of truth.

Joseph Smith of the Mormons claimed that John the Baptist had given to him the priesthood of Aaron. As if this were not enough, he later claimed that he had received a higher priesthood, that of Melchizedek, from Peter, James, and John. His followers repeatedly claim that he has done more for the salvation of this world than any other man who has ever lived, except Jesus.

The late L. Ron Hubbard of the Scientology cult has offered himself as a higher authority than Jesus Christ or the Christian Bible. This science fiction writer has produced a devoted set of followers who have pressed millions of dollars into his hands.

Guru Maharaj Ji has presented himself as the "perfect master" and the "lord of the universe" and is esteemed as such by his thousands of followers across America and the world. It is ironic that this exalted personality, being a juvenile, had to get permission from a local judge to marry his 24-year-old secretary.

Meher Baba of the Bahai cult has said, "There is no doubt of my being God personified...I am the christ. ...I assert unequivocally that I AM infinite consciousness; I make this assertion because I AM infinite consciousness. I am everything and I am beyond everything...Before me was Zoroaster, Krishna, Rama, Buddha, Jesus, and Mohammed...My present avataric form is the last incarnation of the cycle of time, hence my manifestation will be the greatest."

One of the marks of a cult is that it elevates the person and the words of a human leader to a messianic level. The predictable characteristic of a member of a cult is that he will soon be quoting his leader, whether Father Divine, Prophet Jones, Mary Baker Eddy, Judge Rutherford, Herbert Armstrong, or Buddha as a final authority. A messianic human leader has used the powers of his intelligence or personality and with them imposed his ideas and directives on the ignorant.[36]

One does not need much imagination to see what will happen when the light of the world, the church, is removed. Under the cover of spiritual darkness, Antichrist will have no problem successfully deceiving the entire world to agree with him regarding the elimination of God's chosen people, the Jews, and his proclamation to be God.

CHAPTER 14

True and False Unity

Summary

In order for the *world* to become united, the hindering elements such as political, economic, and religious diversity must be dealt with. At the same time, the drive for "Christian" unity is derailing the church from its mission, paving the way for Antichrist. This chapter blows away the smoke, presenting in clear terms what Biblical unity really means.

True and False Unity

In Zephaniah 3:8, we read: *"Therefore wait ye upon me, saith the LORD, until the day that I rise up to the prey: for my determination is to gather the nations, that I may assemble the kingdoms, to pour upon them mine indignation, even all my fierce anger: for all the earth shall be devoured with the fire of my jealousy."*

This verse describes the reason for the gathering of the nations of the world. It is addressed to Israel, telling her she should wait upon the Lord, and be patient, even though she will be persecuted, oppressed, and pressured, until the Lord gathers all the nations for judgment.

While at this point, we do not actually see the gathering of the nations against Israel, Zephaniah, the prophet, saw it 2,600 years ago. The purpose of that gathering is to oppose not only Israel, but in actual fact, *"...against the LORD, and against his anointed..."* (Psalms 2:2). When will that happen? The Battle of Armageddon will be the climax at the end of the Great Tribulation!

The beginning of the gathering of the nations was at the crucifixion of Christ, *"For of a truth against thy holy child Jesus, whom thou hast anointed, both Herod, and Pontius Pilate, with the Gentiles, and the people of Israel, were gathered together"* (Acts 4:27). This Scripture reveals the deeper truth of the crucifixion and the participants. Herod, the half Jew, king of Israel; Pilate, the Roman governor; the gentiles; and finally, Israel. There you have the entire world gathered against the Anointed!

Salvation or Judgment

The nations will be gathered by God and He will pour out *all* His fierce anger upon all the Earth. The purpose is two-fold. First, it is for the salvation of Israel and secondly, it is for the judgment of the world.

A similar event, but on a smaller scale, happened many thousands of years ago when Israel came out of slavery in Egypt. There was a two-fold purpose for that event also: Judgment and destruction of Egypt and the salvation of Israel.

God's Resolutions Never Change

We must never think that in our day God has somehow disassociated Himself from His people Israel, or from the world, or from His church. He permits men to exercise their free will. Men may choose to say "Yes" or "No" to God. He is love and love is only on a free-will basis. This fact, however, does not interfere with the day-to-day development of our world. No matter how the nations, Israel, or the Church of Jesus Christ behave toward God the Creator, His eternal resolutions will never change!

The Love of God

Neither should we ever think that we can change God's resolution through our prayers. When we pray, God will change us, our attitudes, our approach to Him, our thought pattern, and our entire outlook. As soon as we pray, we step into the presence of the Holy God. We will realize, as the prophets of old did, that we are nothing but dust. Thus, we will begin to tremble and weep before the countenance of the Creator. We will experience change, even though the world around us may not change.

We also do well to recognize the good news: In spite of men's rebellion, disobedience and arrogant behavior against their Creator, God still loves men.

The following beautiful verse, found in John 3:16 is a powerful summary of the entire Bible in 25 words: *"For God so loved the world, that he gave his only begotten Son, that whosoever believeth in him should not perish, but have everlasting life."*

Because God is love, He gives. Based on His love, He gives you eternal life. It's a gift which cannot be earned by good deeds, some religious activity, or anything else. It is unconditionally free! Despite this, often we neglect intimate communication with God, thus, we slowly grow cold, losing sight of the fact that God really does love us.

That love of God is incomparable to anything in the history of mankind. And our Lord is long suffering. He is not bound by time as we are. But when His time comes to carry out His resolutions, He commands the fulfillment of His prophecies.

The Gospel Must Be Preached
This is why we continue to proclaim the Gospel of salvation in Jesus Christ to all people, wherever and whenever we have the opportunity we do so. The International Edition of *Midnight Call*, for example, is for people who do not have the financial means to pay for a subscription. They will read the message that God loves them. They are invited to respond to the Gospel, and many do. And Christians are being prepared for the coming of Jesus Christ!

Work Until the Trumpet Sounds
At the moment when the trumpet sounds, it will be too late for anyone to belong to His church if they are not a believer at that time, *"For the Lord himself shall descend from heaven with a shout, with the voice of the archangel, and with the trump of God: and the dead in Christ shall rise first: Then we which are alive and remain shall be caught up together with them in the clouds, to meet the Lord in the air: and so shall we ever be with the Lord"* (1st Thessalonians 4:16–17). It is, therefore, our holy duty to proclaim the Gospel to all men everywhere and by all means possible, as long as there is still time to do so! Based on what we see as far as the fulfillment of Bible prophecy is concerned, there isn't much time left!

Whether we are preachers or teachers, pastors or deacons, choir directors or lay members, we are duty-bound to further the name of Christ with our prayers and financial support. We must work while it is yet day, for the night cometh when no man can work.

The Good and Bad of Evil
The progression of evil, as we experience it in our day, has a negative, but sometimes it also has a positive effect. That is one reason that, as we watch the world become one, we must understand why.

Let us look at what God promised Abraham, who is called the father of all believers. We read, *"And he said unto Abram, Know of a surety that thy seed shall be a stranger in a land that is not theirs, and shall serve them; and they shall afflict them four hundred years."* Verse 16 gives the specific reason for the 400 year captivity: *"But in the fourth generation they shall come hither again: for the iniquity of the Amorites is not yet full"* (Genesis 15:13).

This is an amazing prophecy because Israel did not even exist during the time it was given. The promise was addressed to one person, Abraham, who was childless.

Why 400 Years as Slaves?
Here questions arise, such as, "Why did God lead Israel into slavery for 400 years?" Or, "Why did God not simply kick out the Amorites right away?" We already mentioned that God is love. He had to give the Amorites another chance, an amazing 400 years, until they filled the measure of evil and sin against God.

Remember, while *we* were yet sinners, Christ died for us! During those 400 years, Israel had to learn to be obedient, to become a servant. You can't be obedient to God if you have not learned to be obedient to man. Children are admonished in the

Bible to be obedient to their parents and parents are admonished to be obedient to the government, according to Romans 13.

Israel learned first hand how evil men can be. They were made slaves unto the Egyptians and the Egyptians, in turn, murdered their newborn sons without mercy. That was a lesson never to be forgotten!

Sodom and Gomorrah

Another vivid example of the progression of evil is the story of the cities of Sodom and Gomorrah. The cities were so full of evil that they were marked to be destroyed.

But righteous Lot was a hindering element to God's destruction of those places. So what did God do? Read these amazing words in Genesis 19:22 where an angel sent by God is addressing this urgent message to Lot: *"Haste thee, escape thither; for I cannot do any thing till thou be come thither. Therefore the name of the city was called Zoar."*

I am overwhelmed with the realization of the faithfulness of our loving God! His execution of judgment was hindered by the action of Lot: *"...I cannot do any thing until thou be come thither...."*

The Righteous Lot

Lot was a man who was not ready. He hesitated. Although he is called righteous, his testimony to his family was not very effective: *"And Lot went out, and spake unto his sons in law, which married his daughters, and said, Up, get you out of this place; for the LORD will destroy this city. But he seemed as one that mocked unto his sons in law"* (Genesis 19:14). His own sons in law did not take his warning seriously.

Up until the last moment, Lot still was undecided. We read in the next verse: *"And when the morning arose, then the angels hastened Lot, saying, Arise, take thy wife, and thy two daughters, which are here; lest thou be consumed in the iniquity of the city"* (verse 15).

The angels even had to use physical force: *"And while he lingered, the men laid hold upon his hand, and upon the hand of his wife, and upon the hand of his two daughters; the LORD being merciful unto him: and they brought him forth, and set him without the city"* (verse 16).

When will judgment come upon our world? When the righteous people on Earth are removed! That's another urgent reason why we should begin to make haste, to be ready for the Rapture!

The Church Hindering the Antichrist

In the New Testament, we also find a hindering element for the final progression of evil: the revelation of the Antichrist. In 2nd Thessalonians 2:6–7 we read, *"And now ye know what withholdeth that he might be revealed in his time. For the mystery of iniquity doth already work: only he who now letteth will let, until he be taken out of the way."*

Only after the church, which is the light of the world, is taken "out of the way," can the revelation of the Antichrist take place: *"And then shall that Wicked be revealed, whom the Lord shall consume with the spirit of his mouth, and shall destroy with the brightness of his coming"* (verse 8).

The Antichrist embodies the power of darkness and cannot be revealed in his full capacity of evil while there is still light. Neither can the full power of the wicked one be developed until he has the unity of the people behind him. Revelation 13:8 reads, *"And all that dwell upon the earth shall worship him...."*

This unity will not come about instantaneously, but the preparation for it is in full swing today.

This cannot be fulfilled when the church is present; she must be raptured!

The Perfect Unity of the Church

The ecumenical movement, the World Council of Churches, and various movements and organizations which are trying to unify Christianity are actually working against the will of God. Why? Because the church, the body of believers, is already perfectly unified in the Lord Jesus Christ.

We may attend different denominational or nondenominational churches, or be members of other groups that come together to hear the Word of God and break bread, but we are perfectly united in the Lord Jesus Christ already!

The Fulfilled Unity of the Church

If we are already perfectly one, how do we explain John 17:23, *"I in them, and thou in me that they may be made perfect in one...."* This seems to indicate that Jesus desires the churches to unite. To understand this, we must read previous verses such as verse 20: *"Neither pray I for these alone, but for them also which shall believe on me through their word."* Here we have the revelation that Jesus is prophesying that others will believe on Him through the preaching of His disciples. In John 17, He refers to the idea that "they may be one" four times!

Gentiles Added to the Church

When the Church of Jesus Christ was born on Pentecost, all members were Jews. Later, the gentiles were added and a new problem arose.

Many Jews who believed in Jesus were of the opinion that the gentiles had to become Jews first. In other words, they had to keep the law in order to be saved: *"But there rose up certain of the sect of the Pharisees which believed, saying, That it was needful to circumcise them, and to command them to keep the law of Moses"* (Acts 15:5). The Apostle Paul, however, makes it very plain that their belief was wrong: *"And God, which knoweth the hearts, bare them witness, giving them the Holy*

Ghost, even as he did unto us; And put no difference between us and them, purifying their hearts by faith" (Acts 15:8–9). Thus, gentile believers became one with Jewish believers.

This perfect oneness is later demonstrated by the Apostle Paul when he says in Galatians 3:28, *"There is neither Jew nor Greek, there is neither bond nor free, there is neither male nor female: for ye are all one in Christ Jesus."* This is not something to be achieved in the future. It is a reality here and now, just as it was almost 2,000 years ago during the apostles' time.

Spiritual Unity

It is important to emphasize that this unity is a spiritual union in Christ. It is not applicable to our flesh and blood, nationality, customs, or culture. When the Bible says, *"...there is neither male nor female..."* it doesn't mean that a male ceases to be a male and the female is no longer a female. A Greek is still a Greek, and a Jew continues to be a Jew. So the accusation we often hear from unbelievers that the church is divided because there are so many different denominations is baseless. The Bible speaks of the perfect unity in Christ. Note the last sentence: *"...ye are all one in Christ Jesus."*

This really destroys the philosophy of the ecumenical system, and the many church-oriented, unity-seeking organizations which are attempting to dissolve denominational borders. The differences which exist have no direct relationship to the Church of Jesus Christ.

To summarize, the closer I come to Jesus, the closer I am to my brothers and sisters in the Lord. The unity need not exist in flesh and blood, which would be horizontally, but this unity already exists perfectly in a vertical fashion. What is the difference between horizontal and vertical fellowship? Horizontal means our ties to brothers and sisters in the Lord, whether it be to the east, west, north, or south. This unity is not required because we exist on Earth in our flesh and blood.

The vertical fellowship, however, is spiritual. That is what really counts. In our spirit, we are anchored in one faith to our Lord Jesus Christ who is above sitting at the right hand of the Father.

Unity Must Be Anchored in Jesus

I have experienced this unity many times when traveling to different countries. When we come together with other born-again believers, we don't ask: "Which church or fellowship do you attend? To which group do you belong?" In Jesus Christ, our unity is already perfectly one. Thus our subject is the precious Word of God, the fulfillment of Bible prophecy, the soon-return of the Lord Jesus Christ, or the fact that our task on Earth is almost done.

As Christians, we too should strive for unity, but not as the world does. The goal of such unity must be with one person only, the Lord Jesus Christ. The more you and I are united in the Lord, serving Him with fear and trembling, the closer we are in our fellowship.

Organizational unity is a necessity for a ministry or a church to function. But this type of unity must not be compared to the spiritual unity of the church, which the Bible so clearly speaks of.

The "Perfect Man" Unity

Quite frequently, Ephesians 4:13 is misunderstood, *"Till we all come in the unity of the faith, and of the knowledge of the Son of God, unto a perfect man, unto the measure of the stature of the fulness of Christ."* When we only quote part of the Scripture *"Till we all come in the unity of the faith..."* we can justify the aim and work of the ecumenical movement and its associated groups. But this Scripture specifically emphasizes the individual person *"...unto a perfect man...."* What does this mean? True unity is not measured in how close you are associated with your brother and sister organizationally or in interpretation of doctrine, but perfect true unity is growing in Christ *"...unto a perfect man...."*

This perfect unity of the Church of Jesus Christ is absolutely unique and cannot be imitated. Satan, however, wants to imitate God. Thus, he aims to bring about a one world church.

It is God who is the originator of the different nations, tongues, and people, *"By these were the isles of the Gentiles divided in their lands; every one after his tongue, after their families, in their nations"* (Genesis 10:5). He even divided the land into continents: *"And unto Eber were born two sons: the name of one was Peleg; for in his days was the earth divided; and his brother's name was Joktan"* (Genesis 10:25).

The spirit of transnational, intercultural unity in today's world, therefore, is contrary to God's will. The Church of Jesus Christ is connected to only one earthly people: Israel. The church is God's heavenly people, while Israel is God's earthly people.

While the world's humanistic-based unity will bring forth more prosperity, more comfort, and less chance of war, it is quite obvious from the pages of the Holy Scripture that God has not intended the world to be one. That can only come about on His terms!

CHAPTER 15

How Will the World Become One?

Summary

We discover that democracy, which has produced the greatest peace and prosperity the world has ever known, will spread in a worldwide fashion under Antichrist. It will lead to the introduction of the mark of the beast, which the masses will gladly accept as a path to increased peace and prosperity. We also see that communism failed because of a lack of concern for money, and how credit cards are a first step toward the coming cashless society.

How Will the World Become One?

One of the most difficult things to grasp for citizens who have lived under a free system, such as democracy, is the fact that it will usher in the new age of the Antichrist, a temporary time of world peace and prosperity.

World unity is being accomplished in different ways, and on different levels. An article from the *Kansas City Star*, dated April 26, 1992, gives us an idea of how it is coming together:

> A new economy rules. Because of their different histories and present circumstances, Japan and Europe will be infusing the capitalistic economy with strategies very different from those found in the Anglo-Saxon world.
>
> They will force the economic leaders of the 19th and 20th century, the United Kingdom and the United States, to alter the way they play the economic game. [37]

The new capitalist economy will incorporate different strategies and is indeed altering the traditional economic game the leaders of the world have played thus far.

What we are seeing developing today is unprecedented. The success, as we have previously pointed out, lies in rejecting the old traditional ways and pulling out onto new unknown avenues to achieve prosperity, success, and unity.

For most of this century, the United States has been the world's economic leader. Before the U.S.A., Britain had the power of the world in her hands. If other nations tried to interfere, they were silenced by force.

For example, when the Dutch established New Amsterdam, today's New York, the British simply told them to get out, and they had no choice but to do so.

This type of power wielding was the norm in politics, economy, military, and religion until about the beginning of the 1900's.

The United States, as we previously mentioned, is no longer the undisputed leader of the world. We cannot deny it. Our national debts testify against any other theory. Britain, once a world empire, is now one of the poorer nations of Europe. England's standard of living is substantially lower than that of Switzerland, Sweden, Germany, and Norway, for example. So, just as the *Kansas City Star* article pointed out, the old Anglo-American system is failing and will be superseded by the new social-capital world system now being developed in Europe.

The Coming European World

The new European power structure will fulfill the prophetic predictions which tell us that a one world system will be implemented. When established, it will fall into the hands of an extremely clever person, who Bible scholars call the Antichrist.

The fourth great gentile empire, which is being resurrected today, does not need to be named the Roman world empire. Neither is it necessary to call it the one world order, or new world order.

These and many other names that are being coined now will ultimately merge into one anyway.

Whether the unity of the world is promoted by certain organizations such as the Illuminati, Bilderbergers, the Club of Rome, the G-7, the United Nations, or any other organization, the aim and the result will be the same.

It is not necessary to distinguish between each of them and analyze their objectives because it is the same one world spirit, the same that prompted the building of the Tower of Babel, that is behind them all. Justifiably, we can call the movement towards world unity an unmistakable sign of the endtime.

The Antichrist will be especially successful in the last days when he will incorporate the world into one. This, however, does not necessarily mean everything that is in the world now is evil and must be rejected by Christians, because we are *in* this world but not *of* this world.

All Governments Ordained of God

When analyzing the world, we never must forget that *"...there is no power* [government] *but of God: the powers that be are ordained of God"* (Romans 13:1). If we become politically partial as Christians, then we are participating actively in the political process and we are "of the world." I am fully aware that I will be chided for making such a statement, but I believe that this is Biblical.

Joseph served as a slave in a foreign government and so did Esther.

Of Daniel, we know that he faithfully served two dictatorial governments who destroyed his own country, and led him into captivity.

Above all, Jesus was obedient to the dictatorial oppressive foreign government of Rome!

Governments, whatever they may be, are ordained of God, but each and every one is placed under the jurisdiction of the Devil because he is the god of this world. He is the prince of the powers of darkness. No doubt, there are great differences between the various governments, and surely, the communist governments committed more evil than democratic governments. But these things have no direct relationship to the Church of Jesus Christ.

Using All Things Liberally

While the world is evil, businesses are corrupt and all governments are under the jurisdiction of Satan, the Bible makes it very clear that we can make use of all things liberally in our service to God. Thus we read in 1st Corinthians 3:22, *"Whether Paul, or Apollos, or Cephas, or the world, or life, or death, or things present, or things to come; all are yours."*

We may use all modern facilities, inventions and products for the furtherance of the Gospel and need not analyze everything for hidden diabolical intent.

For example, we have had persons decide not to subscribe to *Midnight Call* magazine for the simple reason that we accept credit cards for payment. It was assumed by these persons that we were therefore in league with the Devil's system. But if we deny the fact that a one world economy already exists, we must be blind.

New Currency

Much has been written about the proposed new money. While in many parts of the world, new money is being issued rather frequently, in the United States, it is almost unthinkable. We have gotten used to the "greenback" for several generations. This is equally true for the British currency. Both, incidentally, are losing purchasing power continuously and there is little doubt by financial experts that one day, they must be replaced with a new currency. In connection with this idea, here is an interesting article:

> The consequences of a universal currency will be simplicity of all arithmetic, operation and facilities gained for travelers, the easing of international transactions and the simplification of exchange rates. When we have a universal currency, trading will receive such a stimulus that it will bypass all the trade records experienced so far. [38]

You would think this is something new, an over-optimistic prediction. If this is your thought, you are dead wrong. This was said in March 1870, by Mr. Feer Herzog, the Swiss Finance Minister in France.

Already at that time, there were those who were dreaming of a unified Europe and a united currency!

World Communism

What is especially unique in our day is the fact that the competing forces of capitalism and communism are being merged
into one since the fall of international communism. The communist system could not compete with capitalism because it
ignored monetary policy.

Back in 1969, in our first issue of the American edition of
Midnight Call, we wrote an article titled, "Communism:
Doomed to Fail." Today, we have witnessed its collapse.

In 1969, it was unthinkable because we heard so much about
the great communist threat. Russia was ahead of the United
States in weapons production, in space travel, and she was
swallowing country after country. The U.S. lost the war against
the small nation of North Vietnam, while the communists
achieved one great victory after another in many parts of the
world.

"Why then," we may ask, "did communism fail?" There
were many reasons, but one specific point that I'd like to mention here is the fact that communism failed to take into consideration that man is basically evil, selfish and loves money.
Capitalism, on the other hand, thrives on "love of money."
During the Reagan years, a book was published using the title,
Greed Is Good.

Anti-God Communism

Communism revealed itself as being anti-God. They loudly
proclaimed "God is dead!" When my mother-in-law was alive,
she frequently went behind the Iron Curtain to visit her relatives in communist East Germany. She never failed to take
along *Midnight Call* literature in spite of the fact that it was
forbidden, and she was caught several times. But the authorities did not arrest her because of her age.

When in East Germany, mom always took the opportunity
to take long walks, especially in the fields of the countryside.

On one occasion, she saw large signs in a wheat field, which had been put up by the communists. The signs read, "Ohne Gott und Sonnenschein bringen wir doch die Ernte ein!" (Without God and sunshine we will still bring the harvest in.) The communists actually challenged God.

Their confidence was strengthened because they had just imported brand new grain harvesters from Russia which were supposedly capable of harvesting wheat during wet seasons, even rain.

Then one day it began to rain, which was not unusual. But the rain continued for seven days. The result was predictable. The crop was flattened. They were unable to harvest the grain even with the most sophisticated Russian machinery.

Overnight, all those signs suddenly disappeared. The communists had taken them away, embarrassed to death.

I don't have to tell you that my mother-in-law, who was a believer, praised the Lord, rejoicing in her heart to see these foolish people defeated by the mighty hand of God.

Anti-Christ Capitalist

The capitalistic system meanwhile is not anti-God, but rather anti-Christ. The system of capital democracy will usher in the Antichrist, therefore, I propose we watch it more carefully in our day.

The communist system was based upon productivity of the worker. Karl Marx, a German Jew, stated in 1848:

> If the workers of the world unite, they will be able to bring forth a paradise on Earth.

But communism failed because it was not centered around the love of money. Instead, they invented their own financial system that was not backed by personal incentives for the individual. But one of the most important ingredients of a workable economy is competition. However, communism rejected it. "All people are equal," they said.

A degree of greediness is essential to make a capitalistic economy work properly. People who are seeking personal wealth generally work a lot more than the average citizen. Many successful businessmen work 12, 14 or even 16 hours a day. Some work 6 to 7 days a week. They are thinking of profit and individual wealth all the time. They are dedicated to success and yes, they do love money.

Believer's Lesson
Believers need to learn a lesson here. We should work day and night, also, but for eternal values. Corruptible gold and silver perish, but precious souls that will be saved through the blood of the Lord Jesus Christ are forever, and they constitute our crown of jewels, our reward for all of eternity.

We all, of course, need money, whether communist, capitalist, or Christian. Midnight Call Ministry could not function without money. We have to pay for printing the magazines, books, and tracts. We need money for wages, for missionaries, and postage.

You and I need money for just about everything. But money should only serve to sustain our standard of living, and most of all, to further the work of the Lord. That is the reason why the Lord gives you health so you can work, make money, and participate in the furtherance of the Gospel.

The Ultimate Control
Money will play a major part in the coming one world system. We read in the last book of the Bible, *"And he causeth all, both small and great, rich and poor, free and bond, to receive a mark in their right hand, or in their foreheads: And that no man might buy or sell, save he that had the mark, or the name of the beast, or the number of his name"* (Revelation 13:16-

17). This is obviously the ultimate system for money control as far as the endtimes are concerned.

The mark of the beast, or the number of his name, will become an absolute financial necessity. I do not believe, however, that this mark will be forced upon people. The general public will recognize the advantage of this system and gladly receive it.

It is significant that worship is mentioned first. The people who will receive the mark of the beast are fully convinced that this is the right thing to do. Why? Because the mark of the beast system will eliminate many of the evils within our society. Think of it: Tax fraud deepens our national debt and places more burden on the honest citizens. The terrible drug trade would receive a death blow at once. Their evil deeds would be crippled because there would be no more cash. Virtually all cash-related crimes would be instantly stopped. Because of these and other obvious benefits, the masses will gladly receive the mark of the beast.

Credit Cards—The First Step Toward Global Money

Today it is necessary to have a credit card if you wish to travel, especially to foreign countries. It would be very difficult for you to make hotel and airplane reservations without one. When you are in a foreign country, the most economic and practical currency is your credit card. It will save you from having to go through the cumbersome process of exchanging your American dollars to local currency, for which the money-changers charge heftily.

We talked about a global currency earlier, and pointed out that the credit card is the beginning of a unified currency. Unfortunately, someone could use it simply by forging your signature. Therefore, it is almost natural for this system to further develop. A credit system that cannot be lost or stolen offers *itself* as security for transactions. A permanent bodily

mark! This global system will be the most successful finan-
cial/political/economic system the world has ever known!

Just think for a moment of the immense amount of money
that could be saved by operating a one world government with
only one military force. Think of the tax cuts, the money freed
for more beneficial uses. It is for that reason the nations of the
world will gladly accept the mark of the beast with the new
world rulership system which promises peace and prosperity
on Earth.

Eternal Unity

But while the world is being united and prepares to welcome
the Antichrist, the father of lies, we believers are, *"Looking for
that blessed hope, and the glorious appearing of the great God
and our Saviour Jesus Christ"* (Titus 2:13). Christians are
being prepared for the coming of the Lord, while the world is
being prepared for the coming of Antichrist.

When Jesus cried on Calvary's cross, almost 2,000 years
ago, *"My God, my God, why hast thou forsaken me?"*, He paid
the price in full for the sins of all mankind. Calvary finished the
payment for sin and unified all of us who believe.

But man's unity in the making in our day is based on his
own intellectual capacity, which is sin-darkened, and subsequently will lead to Armageddon.

From the richest man on Earth, to the poverty-stricken
homeless person, money is still the key word. But whether it
was Sam Walton, [founder of the Wal Mart chain] who was
called the richest man in the world, or the poor homeless fellow living under a bridge, there is no difference at death. The
only thing that counts then is believing in Jesus Christ.

CHAPTER 16

Doomsday Prophecies

Summary

C lean up our Earth, they insist, respect nature, and then world-wide healing will begin. The errors of these and other beliefs are covered here. We see how the world is being led to believe rumors instead of facts.

Global Famine
Exhaustion of Nonrenewable Resources
Skyrocketing Pollution
The Coming Ice Age
Ozone Hole Over Antarctic; U.S.A.
Global Warming

False Doomsday Prophecies

As a vivid example of Satan's lies, let's look at the militant supporters of the environmental movement.

Many of their claims regarding the pollution of the world are based on false information. We will be documenting some of these beliefs.

Of course, we admit the existing problem regarding pollution in the air, in our rivers, and in our streams. And indeed, trees are being cut down in greater volume.

But the fact is that vegetation has increased, rivers and lakes are cleaner and our air is purer than 50 years ago.

People believe that if they fight for a better world, cleaner air, purer water and more vegetation, it will gain them some sort of salvation on Earth. Yet all manner of spiritual, moral, and ethical pollution is tolerated, even encouraged.

It is my opinion that this over-emphasized environmental movement is the Devil's coverup for the real problem man faces, and that is his sin which he refuses to repent of.

But doesn't it seem strange that the world is so united and so resolved when it comes to the ecological status of planet Earth, but they simply ignore the Creator?

The answer is probably found in the fact that most of these people are not Christians. They do not know about the hope of a heavenly home, all that they are concerned with is here and now—this Earth.

Let's take a look now at some false prophecies concerning the environment that have been given in recent years. *The Futurist* (January/February 1995) on pages 14–17, opposed the alarmists by giving scientific answers to the seven most-believed lies about the environment.

It's important to emphasize here that *The Futurist* is not published by a religious organization that believes in the Bible. As a matter of fact, they are not even favorable toward religion. Nevertheless, I would like to share their comments with you:

Seven False Prophecies • 1—Global Famine

"The battle to feed all of humanity is over. In the 1970's the world will undergo famines—hundreds of millions of people are going to starve to death in spite of any crash programs embarked upon now," predicted population alarmist Paul Ehrlich in his book, *The Population Bomb* (1968).

What really happened? While the world's population doubled since World War II, food production tripled. The real price of wheat and corn dropped by 60%, while the price of rice was cut in half.

Seven False Prophecies • 2—Exhaustion of Nonrenewable Resources

In 1972, the Club of Rome's notorious report, *The Limits to Growth*, predicted that at exponential growth rates the world would run out of raw materials—gold by 1981, mercury by 1985, tin by 1987, zinc by 1990, oil by 1992, and copper, lead and natural gas by 1993.

What really happened? Humanity hasn't come close to running out of any mineral resource. Even the World Resources Institute estimates that the average price of all metals and minerals fell by more than 40% between 1970 and 1988. As we all know, falling prices mean that goods are becoming more abundant, not more scarce.

Seven False Prophecies • 3—Skyrocketing Pollution

In 1972, *The Limits to Growth* also predicted that pollution would skyrocket as population and industry increased: "Virtually every pollutant that has been measured as a function of time appears to be increasing exponentially."

What really happened? Since the publication of *The Limits To Growth*, U.S. population has risen 22% and the economy has grown by more than 58%. Yet, instead of increasing as predicted, air pollutants have dramatically declined.

Sulfur dioxide emissions are down 25% and carbon monoxide down 41%. Volatile organic compounds—chief contributors to smog formation—have been reduced by 31%, and total particulates like smoke, soot, and dust have fallen by 59%. Smog dropped by 50% in Los Angeles over the last decade.

Seven False Prophecies • 4—The Coming Ice Age

The public has forgotten that the chief climatological threat being hyped by the eco-doomsters in the 1970's was the beginning of a new ice age. The new ice age was allegedly the result of mankind's polluting haze, which was blocking sunlight.

What really happened? Global temperatures, after declining for 40 years, rebounded in the late 1970's, averting the feared new ice age. But was this cause for rejoicing? NO! Now we are supposed to fear global warming. Freeze or fry, the problem is always viewed as industrial capitalism, and the solution, international socialism.

Seven False Prophecies • 5—Antarctic Ozone Hole

There have been widespread fears that the hole in the ozone layer of the Earth's atmosphere will wipe out life all over the world. John Lynch, program manager of polar aeronomy at the National Science Foundation, declared in 1989, "It's terrifying. If these ozone holes keep growing like this, they'll eventually eat the world."

What really happened? In 1985, British scientists detected reduced levels of stratospheric ozone over Antarctica. Could the Antarctic ozone hole "eventually eat the world"? No, "It is a purely localized phenomenon," according to Guy Brasseur at the National Center for Atmospheric Research. It is thought that the "ozone hole" results from catalytic reactions of some chlorine-based chemicals, which can take place only in high, very cold (below $-80C$, or $-176F$) clouds in the presence of sunlight. It is a transitory phenomenon enduring only a bit more than a month in the astral spring.

Seven False Prophecies • 6—Ozone Hole Over U.S.A.

In 1992, NASA spooked Americans by declaring that an ozone hole like the one over Antarctica could open up over the United States. *Time* magazine showcased the story on its front cover (February 16, 1992), warning that "danger is shining through the sky…No longer is the threat just to our future; the threat is here and now." Then-Senator Albert Gore thundered in Congress, "We have to tell our children that they must redefine their relationship to the sky, and they must begin to think of the sky as a threatening part of their environment."

What really happened? On April 30, 1992, NASA sheepishly admitted that no ozone hole had opened up over the United States. *Time,* far from trumpeting the news on its cover, buried the admission in four lines of text in its May 11 issue. It's no wonder the American public is frightened.

Seven False Prophecies • 7—Global Warming

Global warming is "The Mother of all environmental scares," according to the late political scientist Aaron Wildavsky. Based on climate computer models, eco-doomsters predict that the Earth's average temperature will increase by 4–9 degrees Fahrenheit over the next century due to the "greenhouse effect."

Burning fossil fuels boosts atmospheric carbon dioxide, which traps the sun's heat.

What is really happening? The Earth's average temperature has apparently increased by less than a degree (0.9) Fahrenheit in the last century. And here's more bad news for doomsters: Fifteen years of very precise satellite data show that the planet has actually cooled by 0.13 degrees C.[39]

—The Futurist, Jan-Feb 1995, p. 14–17

How Lies Are Used to Deceive the Masses

False prophecies, rumors, imagination and gossip generate their own energy, but ultimately experience a "burn out."

These doomsday prophecies are a clever attempt by Satan to divert man's attention from the real doomsday: The Great Tribulation that is going to come upon the Earth.

We have banned God from our public places. We don't permit Bible reading and prayer in our schools anymore.

Thus, we are beginning to worship creation more than the Creator. Romans 1:25 mentions those *"...Who changed the truth of God into a lie, and worshiped and served the creature more than the Creator, who is blessed for ever. Amen."*

We are seeing large numbers of the world's population beginning to worship nature, trees, and animals instead of the living God. New Agers are looking inward and adopting an old age religion: They believe that they are somehow God.

Neither the environment nor pollution are the causes of the coming catastrophe. But the refusal to obey the Word of God, and believing the lies of Satan, are the real cause for the coming catastrophe.

Should Christians "Stand Up"?

Unlike the environmentalist who believes in saving this world, discerning Christians are not waiting for the world to get better. They are fully aware the Bible does not teach that.

They are not deluded by the absurd notion that Christians will eventually take over the courts and legislatures. Discerning Christians realize they do not have the Biblical calling to "stand up" in the name of Jesus and politically oppose wickedness in public places.

Christians are preaching the Gospel, calling sinners to repentance and salvation. They are waiting for the Lord Jesus Christ to take them OUT of this world to be present with Him forevermore!

Peter's Admonition is Good for Us Today

I will close this chapter with 2nd Peter 3:11–18, *"Seeing then that all these things shall be dissolved, what manner of persons ought ye to be in all holy conversation and godliness, Looking for and hasting unto the coming of the day of God, wherein the heavens being on fire shall be dissolved, and the elements shall melt with fervent heat?*

"Nevertheless we, according to his promise, look for new heavens and a new earth, wherein dwelleth righteousness. Wherefore, beloved, seeing that ye look for such things, be diligent that ye may be found of him in peace, without spot, and blameless.

"And account that the longsuffering of our Lord is salvation; even as our beloved brother Paul also according to the wisdom given unto him hath written unto you; As also in all his epistles, speaking in them of these things; in which are some things hard to be understood, which they that are unlearned and unstable wrest, as they do also the other scriptures, unto their own destruction.

"Ye therefore, beloved, seeing ye know these things before, beware lest ye also, being led away with the error of the wicked, fall from your own stedfastness. But grow in grace, and in the knowledge of our Lord and Saviour Jesus Christ. To him be glory both now and for ever. Amen."

CHAPTER 17

Democracy: The God of the New Age

Summary

Recent victories of democracy have opened the door for world unity. If democracy is the final system of the gentiles, will it install the Antichrist? How must Christians relate to the coming one world democracy?

Democracy—The God of the New Age

When choosing the title of this chapter, "Democracy—The God of the New Age," I knew that it would be controversial. It may sound as if I am putting down democracy. This, however, is is not my intention at all.

We have experienced democracy as a political system that works best at this moment. It provides certain freedoms unknown heretofore in history. At this time, there is no other viable system comparable to democracy. However, as we investigate it from the Biblical perspective, *we find that democracy, no matter how good, will ultimately install the Antichrist.*

The very fact that today we are experiencing a flood of democracy gives us more reason than ever to believe that the conclusion of the endtime is indeed at hand.

Democracy is on the lips of everyone today, especially since the unexpected, sensational fall of the Iron Curtain. Not one day passes without some report by the news media about the progress of democracy. Some have called democracy the ultimate freedom and liberty for mankind. Others say democracy is the God-given right of everyone on Earth.

Goddess of Democracy

In China, still under communist rule, democracy is considered a religion. During the Chinese student uprising in Tiananmen Square, a paper maché "Statue of Liberty" was displayed. It was called, the "Goddess of Democracy." This is what I want to address in detail, because a goddess or a god of democracy can never be the God of the Bible we worship.

Think of it for a moment. Children educated in communism—and their parents, and grandparents presumably communists—rebelled against the system.

They had to be good communists, otherwise, they would not have been allowed to study at a Chinese university for a higher education. Yet we saw that these students were the ones who put up this "Goddess of Democracy." Were they recognizing something that we as a nation fail to? I think so!

We published an article on the subject in our *News From Israel* magazine in July, 1989, and I quote part of that article here:

> The hope for democracy and the tragedy that followed has been publicized by the news media in detail. What is the significance from the prophetic Word? Geographically, China lies directly east of Israel. Its participation in the endtime scenario is described for us in Revelation 16:12, *"And the sixth angel poured out his vial upon the great river Euphrates; and the water thereof was dried up, that the way of the kings of the east might be prepared."*
>
> Although China is a communist country, they separated themselves from Soviet communism under the leadership of Mao Tse Tung. This did not come as a surprise to students of the Scripture, because China is not categorized within the northern confederacy mentioned by the prophet Ezekiel in chapters 38 and 39. China belongs to the confederacy of kings of the East and therewith to the world empire which is presently arising in Europe.
>
> While the uprisings in the former Soviet bloc countries were based exclusively on materialistic and nationalistic reasons, the uprising in China is different because it includes a religious fervor, as clearly expressed in the "Goddess of Democracy." [40]

Democracy on the March

In the meantime, we have experienced the fall of the Berlin Wall, the symbol that separated East and West, communism and capitalism. Now more than ever, as we witness democracy moving east, rather than communism moving west as feared for so long, it is considered to be the absolute answer to all of the world's problems.

Who can stand in the way of democracy? Just a few years ago, communism was perhaps the most powerful system in the world. Geographically, over half of our planet and about 65% of the world's population was ruled by it.

Now, with this danger to capitalist freedom no longer a real threat, democracy has the stage, front and center. It is the new world power of today. We are approaching the time when no one, absolutely no one, will be able to oppose democracy.

Here we are reminded of Revelation 13:4, *"Who is like unto the beast? who is able to make war with him?"*

While we rejoice in the fact that our brothers and sisters in the Lord in Eastern Europe can gather more freely in fellowship, and we are happy for the liberty they now have to travel to the West, we must not permit this joy to blind us to the new danger that is approaching. *The danger that actually seems so positive is a united world under democracy.*

But who in his right mind could oppose such progress? What's wrong with universal brotherhood, global unity, peace and prosperity? On the surface, nothing, but those who diligently study the Scriptures know exactly what this development will lead to.

Virtually from the beginning, men have been waiting for the right person with the right system which will lead to universal peace and harmony. But, men have wanted it only on their *own* terms. Is peace and prosperity realistically possible in our time? Without hesitance, I would answer "Yes!" Not only is peace possible, but this peace must come because it is prophesied in the Holy Scriptures. Yes, there will be peace at an unprecedented level and it will flood the world in such a way that all opposition will be eliminated.

At the zenith of success, however, it will assume a different face. The gloves will come off and the true nature of it will be revealed. No longer will it move only *horizontally*, that is, globally, but it will begin to move *vertically*, because men want to become as God.

Democracy Cannot Change The Evil Heart

The success of democracy is based on human intellect. But men will be just as wicked as ever before, *"The heart is deceitful above all things, and desperately wicked: who can know it?"* (Jeremiah 17:9).

We know what happened between Adam and Eve's first two sons. An argument arose and one killed the other. Since that time, brother has warred against brother. With absolute certainty, we can be assured that this type of conflict will continue. Wars and rumors of wars, arguments, dissatisfaction, and rebellion will not cease until Jesus comes back again. Only He will bring about true peace.

Regardless of the system of the world's governments, past or present—whether dictatorship, monarchy, democracy, socialism, or communism—all have promised a peaceful and improved life. The goal of virtually all politicians has never changed: They have always assured the people, in effect, "Peace and prosperity for our people, if you elect me...."

Why, then, have we had so many wars? The origin of war is based on hatred. This hatred has not been done away with. It is still deep in the heart of every single person on Earth, unless that person has been bought with the blood of the Lamb, the Lord Jesus Christ. Only then will that individual have real peace which passeth all understanding, and be able to overcome the hatred that so saturates the human mind.

Democratic Dictatorship

The danger of democracy lies in the ironic fact that it will ultimately not tolerate any opposition. The new world democracy of the last days will become, in effect, a world dictatorship.

We found the following in the "Popular Quotations" section of *Webster's Encyclopedic Dictionary of the English Language*:

Democracy means simply the bludgeoning of the people, by the people, for the people.

Winston Churchill, the great British statesman, confessed that:

The worst form of government is democracy, but it's the best we have had.

The point I want to make is that the intoxicating joy that is being expressed today, due to the success of democracy is, in reality, no reason for us to rejoice. In Revelation 16:13–14 we read what it will lead to in the end: *"And I saw three unclean spirits like frogs come out of the mouth of the dragon, and out of the mouth of the beast, and out of the mouth of the false prophet. For they are the spirits of devils, working miracles, which go forth unto the kings of the earth and of the whole world, to gather them to the battle of that great day of God Almighty."* The "unclean spirits" are mightily at work today throughout the world.

For the first time in the history of mankind, it has become possible for a world system to be implemented in order to fulfill Bible prophecy which clearly and distinctly tells us that the entire world will unite. But that is not their *final* goal. In the end, a united world will prepare for battle against God.

On the surface, this is not visible today. No one is talking about fighting God. No person in their right mind would even utter such a thought. But the Scripture we have just read plainly states that the miraculous works accomplished by the nations of the world will have a specific aim: The gathering union against God Almighty.

The Christian's Battle

Today more than ever, Christians must make sure that their position is that of spectators looking over the political field, not down on the turf fighting it out with the pagans. Our goal is to serve the risen and exalted Lord, spreading the liberating Gospel, and to prepare ourselves for His return.

Never must Christians debase themselves by being drawn into things that belong to the world. We must not believe that we are in charge, and that through our activity we can produce world peace, justice and prosperity.

We know with absolute certainty that God controls the world. He installs presidents, prime ministers, kings, and other officials.

Our battle, therefore, is supremely more important than merely controlling or influencing a political system. Because our battle is distinctly *not* with flesh and blood, the Apostle Paul states, *"For we wrestle not against flesh and blood, but against principalities, against powers, against the rulers of the darkness of this world, against spiritual wickedness in high places"* (Ephesians 6:12).

CHAPTER 18

The Time of the Gentiles and Israel

Summary

The arising of the last gentile world empire is the sign by which we can recognize that we are living in the end stages of the end-time. The nations of the world are beginning to establish their own world society of peace and prosperity through social democracy. But parallel to that, God is making His preparation for real peace and the establishment of the coming millennium.

The Time of the Gentiles

We know that the "endtime" began about 2600 years ago, when the first world empire was founded. The Prophet Daniel made it clear: *"Thou, O king, art a king of kings: for the God of heaven hath given thee a kingdom, power, and strength, and glory"* (Daniel 2:37).

Through the Babylonian king, Nebuchadnezzar, God gave us a picture of four different empires. And the fourth, which is the last, would be resurrected. As we have previously mentioned, we are seeing this resurrection literally taking place in our day.

After the prophet Daniel described the four world empires, which were revealed in Nebuchadnezzar's dream, we read in Daniel 2:44: *"And in the days of these kings shall the God of heaven set up a kingdom, which shall never be destroyed: and the kingdom shall not be left to other people, but it shall break in pieces and consume all these kingdoms, and it shall stand for ever."*

Now we see the picture coming together: God is about to set up His kingdom. But He cannot establish the kingdom parallel to the one the world is building, thus, the governments, their systems, and all political identities of the entire world must be done away with.

Israel Must Be Resurrected

At the same time, it was absolutely necessary that Israel be established as an independent nation on the soil promised to their forefathers. The purpose of the establishment of Israel is described for us in the next verse: *"Forasmuch as thou sawest that the stone was cut out of the mountain without hands, and that it brake in pieces the iron, the brass, the clay, the silver, and the gold; the great God hath made known to the king what shall come to pass hereafter: and the dream is certain, and the interpretation thereof sure"* (Daniel 2:45). One thing is clear:

The stone, which is the rock of salvation, the Lord Jesus Christ, came forth from Israel. He must return there again, because He is the very stone which is the threshing instrument of judgment against the nations of the world.

Furthermore, Israel is given to us as an example. In 1st Corinthians 10:6 we read, *"Now these things were our examples...."* So, whatever happened in the past is for the purpose of being an example unto us so we may see and recognize the times in which we live.

God's eternal plan of redemption is to bring personal salvation to the individual, through an individual, His only begotten Son, the Lord Jesus Christ. God's eternal plan of salvation also calls for the liberation of the nations.

Liberation from what? Liberation from dictatorship, from monarchy, from nationalism, from communism, and yes, even from democracy. This will be accomplished through the nation of Israel.

Unfulfilled Peace
The very specific promise for Israel was the coming Messiah. *"And he* [Jesus] *shall reign over the house of Jacob for ever; and of his kingdom there shall be no end"* (Luke 1:33). In spite of this promise, however, Israel is still not saved. The world still has no peace!

The promise of the Scripture is very clear: *"...on earth peace, good will toward men"* (Luke 2:14). And in verse 10, we read: *"...I bring you good tidings of great joy, which shall be to all people."* Indeed, we have to admit that this tremendous heavenly message has not yet been fulfilled on Earth. There is no "peace on Earth."

Neither is there "good will toward men," or "great joy," at least not among the nations. Men continue to fight, argue, and debate. Thus, we know that this part of prophecy will have to be fulfilled yet in the future.

Fulfilled Promise

Read the promise the Lord Jesus Christ gives to His disciples, and therewith to us, in John 14:27: *"Peace I leave with you, my peace I give unto you: not as the world giveth, give I unto you. Let not your heart be troubled, neither let it be afraid."* And in John chapter 16, verse 33 we read: *"These things I have spoken unto you, that in me ye might have peace. In the world ye shall have tribulation: but be of good cheer; I have overcome the world."*

Praise God! What a tremendous message! The most important thing we need to worry about is our personal relationship with Him. Everything else is secondary.

Philippians 4:7 has this promise, *"And the peace of God, which passeth all understanding, shall keep your hearts and minds through Christ Jesus."* Personal peace is available, but not national peace.

Manmade Peace

Now that we have seen what kind of peace God gives, we may ask, "What's wrong with men's attempts toward peace? Is it against God's will for men to bring about peace and live in fellowship and harmony with one another? Are we not admonished in the Bible to live peacefully with one another? Does the Scripture not say *'Blessed are the peacemakers...'*?" (Matthew 5:9). While that is true, the peace which is being produced by man has no relationship to the peace that was brought about by God. Man's peace is temporary.

It is not real because the price for peace is not paid for by man. God is peace. Man sinned against God, thus, man no longer could claim peace.

Subsequently, any human attempts to repair the damage will fail. In this light we understand Ephesians 2:14 better: *"For he is our peace, who hath made both one, and hath broken down the middle wall of partition between us."*

Tower of Babel Democracy

The first attempt at peace through democracy is recorded in Genesis 11:4. No dictator was present. Nor do we read that a king gave a command. The builders of the Tower of Babel were "We the people." They were in charge of their affairs, *"And they said one to another, Go to, let us make brick, and burn them thoroughly. And they had brick for stone, and slime had they for morter. And they said, Go to, let us build us a city and a tower, whose top may reach unto heaven; and let us make us a name, lest we be scattered abroad upon the face of the whole earth"* (Genesis 11:3–4). Democracy was at work!

We know that God confused the languages of the people who were building the Tower of Babel. Why did He do that? The reason was because they wanted to unite themselves against God ultimately.

They were united in their desire to make for themselves a name, not wanting to be scattered upon the face of the Earth. Yet God had specifically instructed the people that they should scatter abroad, and *"...replenish the earth...."* Thus, they acted contrary to the will of God.

The deeper reason for the unity-minded builders of the Tower of Babel was religiously motivated, however. *"...let us build us a city and a tower whose top may reach unto heaven..."* (Genesis 11:4). This is a clear indication that religion, *"...whose top may reach unto heaven..."* was the key in the building of the Tower of Babel. But man is incapable of building a way to heaven. God already accomplished it, but in the reverse direction, not from Earth to heaven, but from heaven to Earth.

Thus, God had to stop the building of the Tower of Babel. He confused the languages of the people and the construction business went bust. They had to leave off in their attempt to finish that tower. Instead they were forced to fulfill God's commandment to *"...replenish the Earth...."*

Calling of One Man

What happened immediately after this episode of democracy in action at the Tower of Babel? God called Abraham. The Bible refers to him as *"...the father of all them that believe...."* God separated him from his family and nation and gave Abraham the promise which was passed down to Isaac, then Jacob, who was later renamed Israel.

Thus we see, right in the beginning, God made it plain that He is against world unity: not integration, but rather segregation. God segregated Abraham from the rest of the world.

In a most remarkable way, the tiny nation of Israel, consisting of only seventy of Abraham's descendants, moved to Egypt where they prospered and increased greatly.

It is quite apparent from the Scripture that the Israelites knew about the blessings and promises given by God to the fathers: Abraham, Isaac, and Jacob.

Segregation, Not Integration

Very remarkable also is the fact that Israel did not integrate with the Egyptians while they were still free. No attempt was made to unite with the people of Egypt.

But when a new Pharaoh, unfamiliar with Joseph, came to power, he made sure that the Israelites would be separated from Egypt. He forced them to become slaves. Here we recognize, again, God's master plan for Israel: Not integration, but separation!

Israel experienced a long period of oppression. During that time, we find no recorded evidence of the divine workings of the God of Israel among His people until Moses. God had everything in His control, nevertheless.

Four hundred years after the promise to Abraham, God commanded Pharaoh through His servant Moses: *"...Let my people go...."* The Bible records in detail the miracles God performed through the hand of Moses in the presence of

Pharaoh to cause him to let Israel go. Ten terrible plagues came upon the land. With the fourth one, God began to act decisively to assure segregation, *"...And I will sever in that day the land of Goshen, in which my people dwell, that no swarms of flies shall be there; to the end thou mayest know that I am the LORD in the midst of the earth. And I will put a division between my people and thy people: to morrow shall this sign be"* (Exodus 8:22–23).

Separation by Blood
Finally, when the tenth and last plague was to be executed upon Egypt, the distinction between Israel and Egypt became even more apparent, *"...And all the firstborn in the land of Egypt shall die, from the firstborn of Pharaoh that sitteth upon his throne, even unto the firstborn of the maidservant that is behind the mill; and all the firstborn of beasts. And there shall be a great cry throughout all the land of Egypt, such as there was none like it, nor shall be like it any more.*

"But against any of the children of Israel shall not a dog move his tongue, against man or beast: that ye may know how that the LORD doth put a difference between the Egyptians and Israel" (Exodus 11:5–7). This is obviously a distinct pronunciation of God's intention for mankind as well: Not democracy, but theocracy; not unity, but separation!

Proof of God Does Not Create Faith
We can barely imagine all the mighty miracles Israel experienced by the hand of God through His servant Moses. Egypt was judged and Israel was saved. The Israelites crossed the Red Sea on dry ground. They were fed quail and manna from heaven in the desert. They drank water from the rock at Mount Horeb. Then there was the defeated enemy, the powerful Amalek, and the mighty miracle of God's audible voice on Mt. Sinai!

Without a shadow of a doubt, God repeatedly demonstrated
to Israel that He is the absolute Almighty. And yet, Israel continued to rebel, and to disbelieve the Word of God!

Today we hear people say, "If I could have just seen the
mighty miracles God did at that time, then I would believe."
No, you would not believe. Even Israel didn't believe. If you
would see all those miracles, it would only strengthen your
flesh and blood, but in the spirit, you would remain empty and
dry. You have the written Word, the Bible. It is God's action.
You can see, experience, and test it for yourself.

The book you have in your hand, from Genesis to
Revelation, is the full counsel of God. You don't need any
additional revelations or miracles to confirm God's love. The
Bible says, *"Now faith is the substance of things hoped for, the
evidence of things not seen"* (Hebrews 11:1). The same Bible
also says, *"...for he that cometh to God must believe that he
is..."* (Hebrews 11:6). Thus, no room is allocated for us to seek
miracles, or supernatural events to confirm our faith, because
"...faith cometh by hearing...the Word of God" (Romans
10:17).

God lamented over those who had seen His mighty miracles
and yet believed not. Neither were they obedient to His Word,
*"Because all those men which have seen my glory, and my mir-
acles, which I did in Egypt and in the wilderness, and have
tempted me now these ten times, and have not hearkened to my
voice"* (Numbers 14:22).

Seducing Miracles

Today, people are seeking miracles. This is why in these endtimes there's so much deception. Many movements claim they
are the recipients of special visions and prophecies. But I say
they are often demonic, camouflaged in Christian terminology.

Matthew chapter 7 records the shocking truth about a group
of people who cast out demons and did great and mighty works

in His name, yet the Lord said, *"...I know you not...ye workers of iniquity"* (Luke 13:27).

I cannot overstate the fact that we must believe in the Lord Jesus Christ according to the Scripture, *"He that believeth on me, as the scripture hath said, out of his belly shall flow rivers of living water"* (John 7:38).

I do not denounce nor reject miracles. I know better. But I am just warning that in these endtimes, especially before the Antichrist will appear, Bible prophecy says there will be mighty signs and miracles performed by the spirit from below to confuse and to deceive mankind.

The Scripture admonishes us to believe by faith rather than by seeing: *"Whom having not seen, ye love; in whom, though now ye see him not, yet believing, ye rejoice with joy unspeakable and full of glory"* (1st Peter 1:8).

Only Moses Believed

In spite of the tremendous acts of God which the people of Israel experienced, they never consistently believed. David later uttered this amazing statement: *"He made known his ways unto Moses, his acts unto the children of Israel"* (Psalm 103:7). Then in Psalm 106:7, he confirms again: *"Our fathers understood not thy wonders in Egypt; they remembered not the multitude of thy mercies; but provoked him at the sea, even at the Red sea."* All the miracles Israel experienced did not strengthen her faith in God, but rather led her along the pathway of rebellion. The unbelievers were forbidden, therefore, to enter the Promised Land.

While their fathers perished in the desert, the children who entered the Promised Land eventually backslid too, *"Then all the elders of Israel gathered themselves together, and came to Samuel unto Ramah, And said unto him, Behold, thou art old, and thy sons walk not in thy ways: now make us a king to judge us like all the nations"* (1st Samuel 8:4–5). Please note that all

the elders came together. Apparently this was a perfect majority. Any politician in the world would wish to have such support today!

"We the People..."

In 1st Samuel 8, we have the record of blatant rebellion against
the living God: *"Then all the elders of Israel gathered themselves together...."* "We the people want to choose our own
king," they said in effect. It was a simple request. *"...Make us
a king to judge us like all the nations."* They did not want to
be separated from the heathens, but desired to be *like* them.

When we read of this event in 1st Samuel, we notice that
God didn't oppose this democratic process. He actually agreed
to it. He gave the commandment unto Samuel: *"...Hearken
unto the voice of the people in all that they say unto thee: for
they have not rejected thee, but they have rejected me, that
I should not reign over them"* (1st Samuel 8:7). God knew
where all this was going to lead. He knew that Israel wanted to
have her own way.

Israel's Quest for Gentile Democracy

In Moses' time, God gathered His people Israel, *"And Moses
brought forth the people out of the camp to meet with God; and
they stood at the nether part of the mount"* (Exodus 19:17).
They had to come out of the camp and meet at a certain place,
for the purpose of hearing God's law. They heard the law but
did not believe!

To summarize, Israel continuously rejected the rulership of
God. Despite the fact that they experienced a multitude of mir-
acles, they still said "No!" to the supreme rulership of God.
That was the great tragedy.

But even after Israel's suffering under the rulership of foreign occupation, she still rejected theocracy. In John 19:15, we
read these very significant and yet sad words, *"...We have no*

king but Caesar." It was democracy in action once again. The multitude of the people rose up against the Lord Jesus Christ. By this action, Israel said "Yes" to the last world dictatorship, the Roman empire, and thereby to the revived Roman empire of today, the European Union!

When we read about the crucifixion of Jesus, we also see that the principle of "the majority rules"—the cardinal principle of democracy—was at work even during that time. The Roman politician Pilate confessed, *"...I find no fault in this man."* Neither could the cruel King Herod accuse Jesus of wrong-doing. After Jesus returned from Herod's presence, Pilate made this statement, *"...I, having examined him before you, have found no fault in this man touching those things whereof ye accuse him: No, nor yet Herod: for I sent you to him; and, lo, nothing worthy of death is done unto him"* (Luke 23:14–15). However, these two powerful politicians were overruled by democracy. Thus, we see that although majority rulership may be preferable, it does not guarantee the execution of righteousness.

Israel Wants Integration
Israel's attempt to be like the gentiles continues until this day. We know from Scripture that her desire will ultimately be fulfilled when Israel is integrated into the European Union—the last Roman world empire.

We must keep in mind when analyzing Israel's history and future, that Jesus prophesied: *"...if another shall come in his own name, him ye will receive"* (John 5:43).

The following is an excerpt from *Midnight Call* magazine, May 1995, page 24:

Israel: One Step Closer To E.U.
Israel appears to be a step closer to associate status in the European Union after France announced it would support

opening E.U. research and development projects to Israeli firms on the same terms given to European companies.

Israel is seeking to upgrade its 1975 trade and economic agreement with the European body by asking for the same associate status as that given to Switzerland and Iceland, which provides economic benefits similar to regular E.U. membership but without voting rights. The E.U. has adopted a friendlier attitude toward Israel since the signing of the Declaration of Principles, particularly in the areas of research and development and agricultural imports.

Israeli Foreign Minister Shimon Peres, in Bonn for meetings with German officials, said if Israel opens its market to Palestinian agricultural products, it is only just that Israel should be compensated.

According to the Jewish Telegraphic Agency, Israel currently has a $5 billion trade deficit with the E.U., its main trading partner.[41]

The Coming False Peace

Israel's population is mainly composed of Jews from around the world. Their intellectual capacity as a nation is unsurpassed. But for the sake of peace and prosperity, Israel is taking great risks by accommodating former sworn enemies into a peace process on paper. Peace is the key word.

If peace can be brought about by these various processes of negotiation, then Israel will come closer to accepting the Antichrist, whom we believe will be a Jewish person with an amazing ability to unite the diverse factions, particularly Jews and Arabs.

Fundamentally, the Arabs hate the people of Israel. Why? Because Israel has received the promise of God and not the Arabs. The Jews are the ones God has chosen for a specific purpose. The Lord Jesus said: *"...salvation is of the Jews"* (John 4:22).

A Forerunner of the Antichrist

Let us, at this point, analyze the person of the Antichrist. During the 30's and 40's, Germany experienced what I believe was the rulership of a forerunner of the Antichrist when Hitler was in power. The first six years were a stunning success.

Out of hopelessness, deep depression, and oppression, Germany stood on her feet and unleashed an industrial powerhouse. She fully utilized the amazing pool of well-educated intellectuals, business people, and craftsmen.

Almost naturally, all opposition was eliminated through the democratic process which resulted in peace, prosperity, and success. The beginning of the downfall became visible only in the midst of the twelve years of Hitler's rulership.

Success of Antichrist

Don't expect the Antichrist to be an evil man, with blood dripping from his mouth, to appear on the world scene fomenting destruction and chaos. Rather, he will be a gentle, kind, compassionate, caring personality who is dedicated to true democracy and is determined to bring peace and prosperity to the world.

I can well imagine that he will support prayer and Bible reading in schools, the political platform of the conservatives, and with a unique ability, he will appease the liberal camp as well. He will be all things to all people. Finally, the world will have a leader capable of taking care of all situations. Most importantly, he will prosper. His policies will actually work and not be empty political promises as our politicians are so fond of making in our day. He will accomplish great things!

Nevertheless, the Antichrist's work is the work of darkness, the Lord's work is the work of light. He shall destroy the Antichrist, the wicked one, with the brightness of His coming: *"...the Lord shall consume with the spirit of his mouth, and shall destroy with the brightness of his coming"* (2nd

Thessalonians 2:8). But until the midpoint of the Tribulation, all of Antichrist's efforts will appear to succeed.

On the Roman Road

One of the first steps towards peace for Israel must be taken in the direction of Rome. The day Israel is accepted in the European Union, peace is virtually assured. Reuters news agency reported the following on December 29, 1993:

> In a landmark step after 2,000 years of strained Christian-Jewish relations, Vatican and Israeli negotiators approved a document in which the Holy See and the Jewish state formally recognize each other.
>
> The document, the most important step in Israeli-Vatican relations since the Jewish state was founded in 1948, was given final approval by delegations which had worked on the accord for 17 months.
>
> Vatican spokesman Joaquin Navarro-Valls said the accord may make it easier for the Vatican to play a greater role in constructing Middle East peace. In the preamble, the Vatican and Israel agree on the singular character and universal significance of the Holy Land.
>
> But in one important article, the Vatican states that while the Catholic Church reserves the right to speak out on moral issues, it agrees not to become directly involved in conflicts.
>
> The agreement says this principle applies specifically to "disputed territories and unsettled borders."
>
> In the same article, both sides commit themselves to support peaceful resolutions to local or world conflicts and to condemn terrorism.
>
> In another article, both sides agree to combat antisemitism, racism, and religious intolerance. The Vatican states it deplores attacks on Jews, desecration of synagogues and cemeteries and acts which offend the memory of the victims of the Holocaust.

Both sides agree to protect freedom of worship and respect each religion's sacred places.

Israel recognizes the Catholic Church's right to run its own schools, communications media and welfare agencies in the Jewish state.[42]

The Power of Money

The amazing success of the new world system, demonstrated uniquely through the European Union, specifically Germany, was brought to light when West Germany, with the power of money, went across the border to East Germany, and literally bought the country for cash! Many predicted gloom and doom, unemployment and a possible collapse of Germany's economy with inflation skyrocketing.

Although unemployment reached threatening proportions, the German mark stood strong. Inflation is under control and the economy healthy. These events, which are taking shape today, are unprecedented. We do not have anything to compare them with in history. Money, merchandise, and monopoly has become the strongest force and the world can no longer oppose it.

Israel Will Be Deceived

Israel cannot exist without being part of the last world empire. She must join herself with the mighty, money-oriented, social-democratic system. Finally, she will experience peace and prosperity. Until when? We read the answer in Daniel 11:36–39, *"And the king shall do according to his will; and he shall exalt himself, and magnify himself above every god, and shall speak marvellous things against the God of gods, and shall prosper till the indignation be accomplished: for that that is determined shall be done. Neither shall he regard the God of his fathers, nor the desire of women, nor regard any god: for he shall magnify himself above all.*

"But in his estate shall he honour the God of forces: and a god whom his fathers knew not shall he honour with gold, and silver, and with precious stones, and pleasant things. Thus shall he do in the most strong holds with a strange god, whom he shall acknowledge and increase with glory: and he shall cause them to rule over many, and shall divide the land for gain."

That's the work of the Antichrist. He will come into power through deception and democracy.

The Time of Jacob's Trouble

But Israel will finally understand what is happening. Her awakening will come at the moment when she sees the Antichrist sitting himself in the temple, declaring himself to be divine, *"Who opposeth and exalteth himself above all that is called God, or that is worshipped; so that he as God sitteth in the temple of God, shewing himself that he is God"* (2nd Thessalonians 2:4).

At that time, God will begin to act on behalf of His own people. Israel will suddenly realize that she has absolutely no hope, and is lost. Then God will initiate His salvation, *"And at that time shall Michael stand up, the great prince which standeth for the children of thy people: and there shall be a time of trouble, such as never was since there was a nation even to that same time: and at that time thy people shall be delivered, every one that shall be found written in the book"* (Daniel 12:1).

That is the beginning of national salvation for Israel. For the first time in all of history, a whole nation will be saved collectively. Finally, Israel will have learned that she cannot save herself. Salvation must come from a higher authority, which is not democracy, but theocracy; not from man, but from God. This salvation will encompass all of Israel.

A Word of Invitation

In the meantime, God is still shouting this message through His servants, in effect saying, "Come to Jesus and be saved!" You must accept the Lord Jesus and His precious blood for the forgiveness of your sins. Nothing else will help you.

As we see these things come to pass—the one world system being formed, the Roman empire resurrected through the European Union, and the nations of the world gathering themselves against one tiny country, Israel—we know that we are living in the end of the endtimes.

The new age has already begun. It is the age that will deceive the entire world with peace, prosperity and *democracy*.

CHAPTER 19

The Great Tribulation and the Day of the Lord

Summary:

Two-thirds of the world population will be killed during the Tribulation. No one will be able to exist without the mark of the beast. An amazing new interpretation of end-time prophecy explains events in detail.

Who Shall Escape The Tribulation?

The Lord Jesus describes the Tribulation with these words: *"For then shall be great tribulation, such as was not since the beginning of the world to this time, no, nor ever shall be"* (Matthew 24:21).

I would like to emphasize that this is not the same tribulation which the world has experienced since the fall of man. Millions upon millions of people are experiencing some type of tribulation, sometimes on a daily basis. We are speaking here of an incomparable catastrophe and destruction the world has never seen.

How can we determine that this Great Tribulation is not something that has happened in the past? Or as some have suggested, that we are already in the beginning of it? Let me quickly enumerate six major points demonstrating that we are not in the time of the Great Tribulation:

- The world is not yet united.
- Mankind is religiously diverse and we have no evidence that Revelation 13:8 is being fulfilled now, *"...all that dwell upon the earth shall worship him."*
- There is no temple in Jerusalem in which the Antichrist can commit *"...the overspreading of abomination."*
- Our leaders do not have "one mind" yet (Revelation 17:13).
- The Lord has not gathered the nations of the world to the Battle of Armageddon.
- The Church of Jesus Christ is still present on Earth.

The Great Tribulation, Prophetically

Throughout the Old Testament, we read of prophecies indicating a terrible day that is to come upon the Earth. It is called *"...the Day of the Lord."* Let us read a few of these Scriptures: *"Howl ye; for the day of the LORD is at hand; it shall come as a destruction from the Almighty"* (Isaiah 13:6).

Fierce Anger

"Behold, the day of the Lord cometh, cruel both with wrath and fierce anger, to lay the land desolate: and he shall destroy the sinners thereof out of it" (Isaiah 13:9).

Vengeance

"For this is the day of the Lord God of hosts, a day of vengeance, that he may avenge him of his adversaries: and the sword shall devour, and it shall be satiate and made drunk with their blood: for the Lord God of hosts hath a sacrifice in the north country by the river Euphrates" (Jeremiah 46:10).

Destruction

"Alas for the day! for the day of the Lord is at hand, and as a destruction from the Almighty shall it come" (Joel 1:15).

The Voice

"The great day of the Lord is near, it is near, and hasteth greatly, even the voice of the day of the Lord: the mighty man shall cry there bitterly" (Zephaniah 1:14).

In reading these few passages, we can sense that this terrible "Day of the Lord" is not some natural catastrophe, or war, not even a World War. Neither is it a form of punishment upon the people on Earth. But this Great Tribulation, "the Day of the Lord," is a judgment unto destruction. Let me explain.

Salvation versus Destruction

Each one of us who are children of God repeatedly experience the Lord's chastising hand, not unto destruction but unto salvation. Hebrews 12 explains the purpose of chastisement, *"And ye have forgotten the exhortation which speaketh unto you as unto children, My son, despise not thou the chastening of the Lord, nor faint when thou art rebuked of him: For whom*

*the Lord loveth he chasteneth, and scourgeth every son whom
he receiveth. If ye endure chastening, God dealeth with you as
with sons; for what son is he whom the father chasteneth not?"*
(Hebrews 12:5–7).

The Scriptures concerning the day of the Lord we have
quoted from the Old Testament do not deal with the love of
God, but rather with "destruction," "fierce anger," and
"vengeance." It is quite apparent that grace is absent on this
"Day of the Lord." Not because God delights in this destructive judgment upon people, but it is the expected execution of
God's righteousness upon unrighteousness.

We must remember that *"God so loved the world, that He
gave His only begotten Son, that whosoever believeth in him
should not perish, but have everlasting life"* (John 3:16). He
has offered this gift patiently for almost 2,000 years. But during these two millennia, the nations of the world collectively
have rejected the only escape from the great destructive tribulation that is coming upon Earth.

The Wrath of the Lamb
Not only did men refuse God's offer of salvation, but when His
wrath comes upon the Earth, we see rebellious reaction by the
people, *"And the kings of the earth, and the great men, and the
rich men, and the chief captains, and the mighty men, and
every bondman, and every free man, hid themselves in the dens
and in the rocks of the mountains; And said to the mountains
and rocks, Fall on us, and hide us from the face of him that sitteth on the throne, and from the wrath of the Lamb"*
(Revelation 6:15–16).

Interestingly, the religious people will begin to pray, not to
Jesus, but to the rocks and mountains to hide them from the
presence of the *"...wrath of the Lamb."*

No longer is the blood of the Lamb of God active for these
people. The time of grace has passed. He who could have been

the salvation of each and every person on Earth now becomes their judge!

It is something most unusual because a lamb is a meek animal, very lowly, and not aggressive. It follows patiently in the footsteps of the shepherd. Now we see the other side of the Lamb of God.

The people who in vain attempt to escape do not see the Lion of the tribe of Judah, but rather the wrath of the Lamb. This is extremely significant. Those who have rejected the free offer of salvation will be confronted with the Savior, the Lamb of God, who could have saved them. But it will be too late.

Refusal to Repent

Later in the book of Revelation, we read that repentance will be nonexistent: *"And the rest of the men which were not killed by these plagues yet repented not of the works of their hands, that they should not worship devils, and idols of gold, and silver, and brass, and stone, and of wood: which neither can see, nor hear, nor walk: Neither repented they of their murders, nor of their sorceries, nor of their fornication, nor of their thefts"* (Revelation 9:20–21). Mankind will be involved in the manufacturing of their own gods to the extent that it becomes virtually impossible for them to believe anything else. Here we see 2nd Thessalonians 2:11 fulfilled: *"And for this cause God shall send them strong delusion, that they should believe a lie."*

The Ultimate Blasphemers

As if it were not enough that these men will try to hide from the presence of the wrath of the Lamb and refuse to repent, they blaspheme the very God who has the power over destructive punishment. In Revelation 16 we read, *"And men were scorched with great heat, and blasphemed the name of God, which hath power over these plagues: and they repented not to give him glory. And the fifth angel poured out his vial upon the seat of the beast; and his kingdom was full of darkness; and they gnawed their tongues for pain,*

"And blasphemed the God of heaven because of their pains and their sores, and repented not of their deeds" (verses 9–11).

The Purpose of The Great Tribulation

We have already determined that the Tribulation is the implementation of God's destructive judgment upon a rebellious humanity. The Tribulation will be the climax of the confrontation between light and darkness, truth and lies, life and death, salvation and destruction. The purpose for the Tribulation, therefore, is the destruction of the gentile democratic world system. But there is another key purpose for the Great Tribulation: The salvation of His people, Israel.

The prophets Ezekiel and Obadiah both emphasized that the Day of the Lord is directed towards the heathen: *"For the day is near, even the day of the LORD is near, a cloudy day; it shall be the time of the heathen"* (Ezekiel 30:3).

"For the day of the LORD is near upon all the heathen: as thou hast done, it shall be done unto thee: thy reward shall return upon thine own head" (Obadiah 1:15).

Why will this destructive judgment not be directed towards the people of Israel? Because it was only the Jews who have been blinded by God and became enemies of the Gospel for the sake of the gentiles. Romans 11:28 says, *"As concerning the gospel, they are enemies for your sakes: but as touching the election, they are beloved for the fathers sakes."*

Gentiles to Comfort Israel

Although the Jews *"...are the enemies of the Gospel,"* we must remember that it is for *our* sakes. Therefore, we must note the Old Testament admonition which is addressed to the gentiles concerning Israel: *"Comfort ye, comfort ye my people, saith your God. Speak ye comfortably to Jerusalem, and cry unto her, that her warfare is accomplished, that her iniquity is pardoned: for she hath received of the LORD'S hand double for all her sins"* (Isaiah 40:1–2). God is admonishing the gentiles to comfort Jerusalem, to speak favorably towards His people who have received a double portion of punishment for sins.

Double Portion of Punishment Prophesied

Quite obviously, this did not take place during the time of the Babylonian captivity. In Ezra 9:13, we read of the confession of the people, *"And after all that is come upon us for our evil deeds, and for our great trespass, seeing that thou our God hast punished us less than our iniquities deserve, and hast given us such deliverance as this."* At that time, the Jews had not received a double portion of punishment, but less than they deserved! That's their own confession!

The prophets Isaiah and Jeremiah predicted a double portion of punishment, *"For your shame ye shall have double; and for confusion they shall rejoice in their portion: therefore in their land they shall possess the double: everlasting joy shall be unto them"* (Isaiah 61:7). *"And first I will recompense their iniquity and their sin double; because they have defiled my land, they have filled mine inheritance with the carcases of their detestable and abominable things"* (Jeremiah 16:18).

Therefore, we must come to the conclusion that between the return from Babylonian captivity and their final return to the land of Israel in the 1900's, the Jews have received a double portion of punishment for their sins.

14 Million Jews Killed

Think about A.D. 70 when the temple was destroyed and a great multitude of Jews were killed by the Romans. What about the infamous Spanish Inquisition and the repeated killing of Jews throughout Europe during the Middle Ages, especially during the Papal crusades! And finally, consider the Holocaust, during which over six million Jews were ruthlessly murdered under the rulership of Nazi Germany.

Jewish Historians Claim that Over 14 Million Jews Were Murdered Since A.D. 70
Thus the question arises, "Have the gentile nations comforted the Jews and Jerusalem as God commanded?" Not at all! As a matter of fact, the world has never been so united, as it is today, in its opposition to Israel and the land God gave to them.

Gentiles Parting the Holy Land
This is another reason, writes the prophet Joel, for the destructive Tribulation upon the gentile nations: *"I will also gather all nations, and will bring them down into the valley of Jehoshaphat, and will plead with them there for my people and for my heritage Israel, whom they have scattered among the nations, and parted my land"* (Joel 3:2). Interestingly enough, it says "all nations." They indeed parted the land which God calls "my land."

We see the same distinction between these two types of judgments through the Great Tribulation in Isaiah 60:2, *"For, behold, the darkness shall cover the earth, and gross darkness the people: but the LORD shall arise upon thee, and his glory shall be seen upon thee."*

Jerusalem the Stumbling Stone
As if this is not enough, the nations are occupied, not only with the land of Israel, but with the city of God, the city of Jerusalem. Here is what the prophet Zechariah has to say about it, *"Behold, I will make Jerusalem a cup of trembling unto all the people round about, when they shall be in the siege both against Judah and against Jerusalem. And in that day will I make Jerusalem a burdensome stone for all people: all that burden themselves with it shall be cut in pieces, though all the*

people of the earth be gathered together against it" (Zechariah 12:2–3).

Now we see the admonishment given in Isaiah 40:1–2 in a different light. The gentile nations do exactly the opposite of God's command to comfort the Jews and Jerusalem!

Israel's Hope in Destruction

When the greatest and most terrible time comes upon Earth, specifically for Israel, they will experience such tribulation as never before, but in the moment of utter devastation, when there is no more hope, when all seems to be lost, suddenly Israel's unexpected hope will be realized, *"And it shall come to pass in that day, that I will seek to destroy all the nations that come against Jerusalem. And I will pour upon the house of David, and upon the inhabitants of Jerusalem, the spirit of grace and of supplications: and they shall look upon me whom they have pierced, and they shall mourn for him, as one mourneth for his only son, and shall be in bitterness for him, as one that is in bitterness for his firstborn"* (Zechariah 12:9–10).

Therewith, we have established the first group of people who will escape the destructive judgment of the Great Tribulation: Israel!

Two-Thirds of the World's Population Will Be Killed

The church, which is the hindering element for the Great Tribulation, will also escape in accordance with 1st Thessalonians 5:9, *"For God hath not appointed us to wrath, but to obtain salvation by our Lord Jesus Christ."*

The world's population will be reduced drastically, to about one-third. From the remnant of the gentiles who have survived the apocalyptic catastrophes, many will enter into the thousand-year Kingdom of Peace.

We must see one thing clearly. The moment the Great Tribulation has come to an end, the millennium will not be implemented instantaneously for all nations, but it will take a process of time. Nevertheless, the end of the Great Tribulation is caused by the physical appearance of the Lord Jesus Christ on the Mount of Olives and from there, Jesus is in charge.

Then, the remnant of the nations will be categorized and judged according to their works. But this has no relationship to eternal salvation, for we are dealing now with earthly things. The government of our Lord will be executed from the city of Jerusalem in Israel.

Egypt to be Judged
We can see this, for example, regarding Egypt. The prophesied judgment of Ezekiel 29 has not taken place, *"Therefore thus saith the Lord GOD; Behold, I will bring a sword upon thee, and cut off man and beast out of thee. And the land of Egypt shall be desolate and waste; and they shall know that I am the LORD: because he hath said, The river is mine, and I have made it. Behold, therefore I am against thee, and against thy rivers, and I will make the land of Egypt utterly waste and desolate, from the tower of Syene even unto the border of Ethiopia. No foot of man shall pass through it, nor foot of beast shall pass through it, neither shall it be inhabited forty years.*

"And I will make the land of Egypt desolate in the midst of the countries that are desolate, and her cities among the cities that are laid waste shall be desolate forty years: and I will scatter the Egyptians among the nations, and will disperse them through the countries. Yet thus saith the Lord GOD; At the end of forty years will I gather the Egyptians from the people whither they were scattered" (verses 8–13). Egypt will experience this before it enters into the millennium of peace.

The Real Escape
There is a wonderful, indescribable and glorious assurance, namely, that you can escape now, at this moment. You can have

the absolute assurance of being in the presence of the Lord for eternity. The only way to escape is through a person who declares, *"I am the way!"* He is the truth. He is the light of the world. He is Jesus, the Son of the Living God. When you believe in Him, you have passed *"...out of darkness into His marvelous light"* (1st Peter 2:9).

Read the promise of Romans 8:1, *"There is therefore now no condemnation to them which are in Christ Jesus, who walk not after the flesh, but after the Spirit."*

How can you belong to this select group? The answer is almost too simple: Come to Jesus, confess your sins and thank Him that He has poured out His precious blood for your sins and has made you a child of God for all eternity. John 3:36 testifies, *"He that believeth on the Son hath everlasting life: and he that believeth not the Son shall not see life; but the wrath of God abideth on him."*

This is the real escape! Salvation can only come through Jesus Christ. And when you accept Him as your personal Savior, you will belong to the Church of Jesus Christ!

CHAPTER 20

Countdown to the Rapture

Summary:

The end stages of the endtime have begun. Because the Great Tribulation is not far off, we must identify the events that must take place so the implementation of the separation of Israel and the church can occur. The two parts of the Tribulation are expounded and the "fallen tabernacle of David" identified.

The Great Tribulation

When will the Great Tribulation start? In recent years, several messages have come across my desk which argue that the time period of the Great Tribulation is not seven, but only three-and-a-half years in duration. The articles state that nowhere in the Bible do we read that the time period of the Great Tribulation is seven years.

To establish a rebuttal to this claim, we must first answer the question: "What makes the Great Tribulation recognizable?" For one, *"...darkness shall cover the earth..."* as we read in Isaiah 60:2. And why will it be dark? Because the light, the church, has been removed. Jesus said, *"Ye are the light of the world..."* (Matthew 5:14).

The reason we as Christians are the light of the world is due to the fact that we are one with Jesus who said: *"...I am the light of the world: he that followeth me shall not walk in darkness, but shall have the light of life"* (John 8:12). Therefore, to answer the question regarding the length of the Great Tribulation, we must take a closer look at the hindering element, which is the church.

Rapture: Beginning of the Countdown

The church will be taken out of the world in an event known as the Rapture. The Bible states that the Rapture will occur at a time *"...when ye think not"* (Luke 12:40). Suddenly, unexpectedly, and without any announcement, the Lord will come. Therefore, we cannot pinpoint the beginning of the Great Tribulation because we cannot predict the time of the Rapture.

We do know, however, that the moment the church is taken out of this world, the light is gone and darkness will preside over Earth. Then the powers of darkness will have their heyday. The people left behind will do as they please because the light is not there to expose their wickedness any longer. Everything that is of God will then be done away with.

The Antichrist—Daniel calls him *"...a king of fierce countenance, and understanding dark sentences..."*—will fulfill his intentions unhindered because the church is gone.

What Is The Rapture?

Someone may be unfamiliar with the term, "Rapture." It is not found in our major English translations of our Bible. While much is being written about this subject and many theologians are beginning to oppose the reality of the Rapture, let us just read two verses that clearly and distinctly speak about the taking away of the church, *"For the Lord himself shall descend from heaven with a shout, with the voice of the archangel, and with the trump of God: and the dead in Christ shall rise first: Then we which are alive and remain shall be caught up together with them in the clouds, to meet the Lord in the air: and so shall we ever be with the Lord"* (1st Thessalonians 4:16–17).

There is no indication whatsoever revealing the time of our departure. The Bible simply concludes, *"Wherefore comfort one another with these words"* (verse 18). We don't need to have a Ph.D. to understand that Paul is referring here to the preceding verses explaining the Rapture and now states that waiting for this event is our comfort.

There is no doubt that throughout two millennia, numerous Christians who lived under persecution and faced severe punishment and often death, did indeed hold fast to the comfort that Jesus could come at any moment.

The Church And Israel

Before we go on, we must point out that there is an exclusive *difference* between the Church of Jesus Christ and the nation of Israel. If Israel is God's chosen people, and they are in the Tribulation, would they not be considered a light unto the world? Let's look at the answer in the Word of God.

During the first apostolic council in Jerusalem, according to Acts 15, we read about the declaration of an amazing prophecy. The purpose of the gathering was to discuss the membership of the gentiles in the church because there was some confusion about the distinction between the Jews and gentiles.

We quickly find out that this type of a church business meeting was much like the ones we experience in our day. In verse 7 we read, *"And when there had been much disputing..."*, clearly revealing the disagreement within the church.

Finally, however, we read in verses 13–14, *"...after they had held their peace, James answered, saying, Men and brethren, hearken unto me: Simeon hath declared how God at the first did visit the Gentiles, to take out of them a people for his name."* James repeats the message Peter had declared previously and adds, *"And to this agree the words of the prophets; as it is written"* (verse 15). Here, a determination is being made based on the Bible. It agrees with the prophets. They surely believed the written Word of God!

Separation By the Tabernacle

Now comes the revelation of the *distinction* between Israel and the church, *"After this I will return, and will build again the tabernacle of David, which is fallen down; and I will build again the ruins thereof, and I will set it up"* (verse 16). In verse 14, God has taken out from among the gentiles a people for His Name, which is the church, and here in verse 16, He is returning to Israel and rebuilding her.

Our heavenly Father has been taking out from among the gentiles a people for his name for almost 2,000 years. I do believe that this selection is almost complete. Why? Because the reappearance of Israel has become a reality. Any day, we can expect the last one from among the gentiles to be added, and therewith, the number will be complete and the church will be raptured!

The Fallen Tabernacle of David

Has God already begun to resurrect the "fallen tabernacle of David?" To answer this question, we must ask, "What is this 'fallen tabernacle of David?'" James was quoting Amos 9:11, which reads, *"In that day will I raise up the tabernacle of David that is fallen, and close up the breaches thereof; and I will raise up his ruins, and I will build it as in the days of old."*

This tabernacle is not to be confused with the tabernacle-tent which David had pitched to house the Ark of the Covenant: *"And they brought in the ark of the LORD, and set it in his place, in the midst of the tabernacle that David had pitched for it: and David offered burnt offerings and peace offerings before the LORD"* (2nd Samuel 6:17).

Acts 15:16 reads, *"...and I will build again the ruins thereof...."* Ruins in general refer to stones that were thrown about, broken down and in need of reassembly. But because there never was a "tabernacle of David," made from stones, we know that Acts 15:16 does not speak of a literal tent-like taber-nacle. Thus, this "fallen tabernacle" is nothing other than the national identity of the nation of Israel!

More Than One Tabernacle?

How do we know for sure that Acts 15:16 does not speak of the *literal* tabernacle? Let's look at an example: During David's time, there was a justifiable debate regarding which tribe should be the main tribe, the one that should execute the deci-sive leadership for all the tribes of Israel. Logically, some prob-ably thought it should be Joseph because he was the one responsible for saving his brethren and establishing the nation of Israel in Egypt. But the Bible clearly states, *"Moreover he [God] refused the tabernacle of Joseph, and chose not the tribe of Ephraim"* (Psalm 78:67). Here we clearly see that the word "tabernacle" does not exclusively refer to the tabernacle of the Ark of the Covenant.

Furthermore we read in Amos 9:12, *"That they* [Israel] *may possess the remnant of Edom, and of all the heathen, which are called by my name, saith the Lord that doeth this."* Here He identifies the relationship between Israel and the church, *"...and of all the heathen, which are called by my name."*

The Church and Israel Are Organically One

Although Israel and the church are distinctively different identities, they belong organically together. Romans 11 makes this very plain. As gentiles, we are, contrary to nature, grafted into the natural olive tree, which is Israel, *"For if thou wert cut out of the olive tree which is wild by nature, and wert graffed contrary to nature into a good olive tree: how much more shall these, which be the natural branches, be graffed into their own olive tree?"* (Romans 11:24). Thus, Christians from among the gentiles are one with Israel. The church and Israel have the same roots.

To summarize, the resurrection of David's fallen tabernacle is the return of the Jewish people to their land in our day. Realizing that these things are happening now, we cannot but come to the conclusion that the time of the church is coming to an end.

Not only is the Church of Jesus Christ connected with Israel, but Israel's salvation is connected to the fulness of the gentiles. Paul writes to the Romans, *"...blindness in part is happened to Israel, until the fulness of the Gentiles be come in. And so all Israel shall be saved..."* (Romans 11:25–26).

Seven Years of Great Tribulation

The fact the Israel is increasing in stature in our day is an additional sign for the church that the Rapture is close and therewith we are nearing the beginning of the Great Tribulation.

The moment when Israel is integrated into the European Union, which we have identified as the resurrected Roman empire, and have become part of the world family of nations, they in fact have then refused to be a peculiar people chosen by God. I believe *that* is the beginning of the Antichrist covenant.

The prophet Daniel describes a document, or covenant, which will initiate the beginning of the Great Tribulation, *"And he shall confirm the covenant with many for one week: and in the midst of the week he shall cause the sacrifice and the oblation to cease, and for the overspreading of abominations he shall make it desolate, even until the consummation, and that determined shall be poured upon the desolate"* (Daniel 9:27).

Here we have a time span which is clearly given for the Great Tribulation: "One week." Based on Daniel 9, verses 24–26, we know that this "week" means seven years. Each day represents one year.

How do we know this? From verse 24, where the Angel Gabriel tells Daniel that *"Seventy weeks are determined upon thy people and upon thy holy city, to finish the transgression, and to make an end of sins, and to make reconciliation for iniquity, and to bring in everlasting righteousness...."* Seventy times seven equals 490. From the commandment to restore Jerusalem to the accomplishment of reconciliation for iniquity through the Lord Jesus Christ on Calvary's cross, was 483 years. That leaves seven years for the Tribulation period, ending in the arrival of everlasting righteousness!

Someone may now ask, "What happened to the almost 2,000 years since that time?" Daniel writes about the crucifixion in his prophetic timetable, *"...after three score and two weeks shall Messiah be cut off, but not for himself...."* Luther translates this, *"After sixty-two weeks, the anointed shall be destroyed and nothing shall be."* And the Hebrew Bible states, *"After those sixty-two weeks, the anointed will disappear and vanish."* Interestingly enough, in the margin of the Hebrew Bible, the explanation for "the anointed will disappear" is given as "meaning in Hebrew uncertain." But that meaning is

very plain. The anointed shall be in the presence of the Father
for about 2,000 years, absent from Israel—vanished!

The Second Part of the Tribulation
It is important to realize that the Bible concerns itself mainly
with the second half of the Great Tribulation. The first three
and a half years will be absolutely glorious. Men will pride
themselves with the indescribable achievement of peace and
prosperity the world over. Wherever and whenever conflicts
arise, they will be solved quickly. How do we know this?
Under the rulership of the Antichrist, there is little, if any,
chance for opposition because the Bible says, *"...who is able
to make war with him?"* (Revelation 13:4).

The False Peace
The people will remember all the wars, the strife, the conflict,
bloodshed, and unrighteousness that was committed for thousands of years, but, they will believe that it has finally come to
an end. Politicians the world over will proudly proclaim, in the
shadow of Great Britain's Neville Chamberlain as he exited a
meeting with Hitler, "Peace in our time!" The conflict between
the nations, states and races of people will be solved. Religious
leaders will extol their systems for bringing peace to the world.
There will be no difference between Catholics and Protestants,
Jews and Moslems, Hindus or Buddhists. They will all be one,
rejoicing in peace, and giving honor and glory to their gods.
All religions of the world will be brought under one unifying
roof. The masses will decide that there is but one god,
(although they will pick the false one) who may be worshiped
by different names.

New Religion
If such a future is difficult for you to comprehend, especially
in light of all the religious conflict we see today, then you

should read the following release, which is now over twenty years old:

Buddhists, Christians, Confucianists, Hindus, Jains, Jews, Muslims, Shintoists, Sikhs, Zoroastrians and still others, we have sought here to listen to the spirit within our varied and venerable religious traditions...We have grappled with the towering issues that our societies must resolve in order to bring about peace, justice, and an ennobling quality of life for every person, and every people...We rejoice that... the long era of prideful, and even prejudiced isolation of the religions of humanity is, we hope, gone forever. We appeal to the religious communities of the world to inculcate the attitude of planetary citizenship.[43]

—The Louvain Declaration from the Second World Conference on Religion and Peace under Catholic Leadership. *Catholic Register*, Toronto, Canada, Sept. 1974)

The Pride of Antichrist

Opposition will not be tolerated in such a new world order because of the Antichrist's amazing success. His prosperity is again emphasized in Daniel 11:36, *"...the king shall do according to his will; and he shall exalt himself, and magnify himself above every god, and shall speak marvellous things against the God of gods, and shall prosper till the indignation be accomplished: for that that is determined shall be done."*

But, his pride will cause the beginning of his downfall. After three-and-a-half years of unprecedented success, the Antichrist will declare himself to be God. 2nd Thessalonians 2:4 confirms him as the one *"Who opposeth and exalteth himself above all that is called God, or that is worshipped; so that he as God sitteth in the temple of God, shewing himself that he is God."*

Then the second half of the Great Tribulation will begin. How do we know this? Daniel gives us the answer, *"And he*

[Antichrist] *shall confirm the covenant with many for one week and in the midst of the week: he shall cause the sacrifice and oblation to cease..."* (Daniel 9:27). Knowing that a "week" means seven years, the "midst" of it is three-and-a-half years.

At that time, Israel will finally recognize that he is not the promised Messiah. He will declare himself to be God, and the Jews know that a man cannot be God. But it is not Israel who breaks the covenant. The Antichrist does, *"He hath put forth his hands against such as be at peace with him: he hath broken his covenant"* (Psalm 55:20).

The End of the Great Tribulation

The second half of the Great Tribulation is also marked by the Antichrist's special hatred for the God of heaven, *"And he shall speak great words against the most High, and shall wear out the saints of the most High, and think to change times and laws: and they shall be given into his hand until a time and times and the dividing of time"* (Daniel 7:25). We see that a very definite time limit is stated, *"...a time and times and the dividing of time."* In plain English, one year, plus two years, and half-a-year makes three-and-a-half years!

The beginning of the second half is marked by the taking away of the sacrifice in the rebuilt temple in Jerusalem and the proclamation of the Antichrist to be God, which leads to his request to be worshiped: *"Yea, he magnified himself even to the prince of the host, and by him the daily sacrifice was taken away, and the place of the sanctuary was cast down. And an host was given him against the daily sacrifice by reason of transgression, and it cast down the truth to the ground; and it practised, and prospered"* (Daniel 8:11–12). Even throughout the last half of the Great Tribulation, he continues to prosper.

Now, no one is able to stop him. He has all the power in his hand and considers himself to be God, *"Even him, whose coming is after the working of Satan with all power and signs and lying wonders, And with all deceivableness of unrighteousness in them that perish; because they received not the love of the truth, that they might be saved"* (2nd Thessalonians 2:9–10). For all practical purposes, the Antichrist will become the supreme ruler of the world.

Only Israel will oppose him, and as a result, she will be persecuted so severely that God has to intervene supernaturally to protect His people, *"And to the woman were given two wings of a great eagle, that she might fly into the wilderness, into her place, where she is nourished for a time, and times, and half a time, from the face of the serpent"* (Revelation 12:14).

Again we see the description, *"...a time, and times, and half a time...",* meaning three-and-a-half years. When this time is up, then the Lord will make an end of the powers of darkness with His appearance. This is recorded in 2nd Thessalonians 2:8, *"And then shall that Wicked be revealed, whom the Lord shall consume with the spirit of his mouth, and shall destroy with the brightness of his coming."* That is the ending of the Great Tribulation!

CHAPTER 21

The Millennium: Beginning and Ending

Summary:

Satan's kingdom and his power will be ended by the Victor, the Lord Jesus Christ. This chapter reveals Satan's origin and his ultimate destination. We also give a revealing interpretation on "Gog and Magog" and the mark of the beast.

Who Shall Populate the Millennium?

In the first seven verses of Revelation 20, we find the documentation for the thousand-year kingdom of peace. We will emphasize, to begin with, four important subjects:

- The arrest, conviction, and sentencing of the deceiver, the hindering element for genuine peace.

- Believers who come out of the Great Tribulation and rule with Christ a thousand years.

- The first resurrection and the abolishment of the second death for those who are part of the first resurrection.

- Satan's temporary release and final end.

"And I saw an angel come down from heaven, having the key of the bottomless pit and a great chain in his hand. And he laid hold on the dragon, that old serpent, which is the Devil, and Satan, and bound him a thousand years,

"And cast him into the bottomless pit, and shut him up, and set a seal upon him, that he should deceive the nations no more, till the thousand years should be fulfilled: and after that he must be loosed a little season. And I saw thrones, and they sat upon them, and judgment was given unto them: and I saw the souls of them that were beheaded for the witness of Jesus, and for the word of God, and which had not worshipped the beast, neither his image, neither had received his mark upon their foreheads, or in their hands; and they lived and reigned with Christ a thousand years.

"But the rest of the dead lived not again until the thousand years were finished. This is the first resurrection. Blessed and holy is he that hath part in the first resurrection: on such the second death hath no power, but they shall be priests of God

and of Christ, and shall reign with him a thousand years. And when the thousand years are expired, Satan shall be loosed out of his prison" (Revelation 20:1–7).

Satan's Arrest

In the above Scripture, we see that the angel who comes down from heaven is not confronting the dragon. There is no battle here and no resistance.

This is strictly the arrest of Satan, also known as the dragon, the old serpent, the Devil. We simply read, *"...and he* [the angel] *laid hold on the dragon...."* Satan is securely bound and cast into the bottomless pit whereupon a seal is set so he cannot escape and deceive the nations.

We may ask, "Why did Satan not resist his arrest?" After all, he is the great rebellious one. We could well imagine that his refusal to cooperate would cause quite a problem.

The fact that he had to be "taken" and "laid hold on" shows that he is now powerless. But that he had to be "bound" indicates this is not the final judgment and that the Devil still harbors a potential danger.

The reason the angel does not need to fight is based on the fact that Satan is a defeated foe. At the appearance of the Lord Jesus, his lying and deceptive nature will be exposed and therewith he will be stripped of his power in the presence of the Omnipotent.

The Apostle Paul describes this in just one verse in 2nd Thessalonians 2:8, *"And then shall that Wicked be revealed, whom the Lord shall consume with the spirit of his mouth, and shall destroy with the brightness of his coming."* Note that the Lord will not defeat Satan "...with His power..." but destroy him with *"...the brightness of His coming."*

Jesus is the light of the world. Where the Lord is, there is no darkness. Nothing can be hidden. He has eyes like *"...a flame of fire..."* Revelation 1:14 tells us.

It is this same Jesus of whom John testified—that He is the light of men, *"In him was life; and the life was the light of men"* (John 1:4). But this light was rejected because of the deceptive activity of Satan so that men would not see the light, but remain in darkness. Thus verse 5 says, *"And the light shineth in darkness; and the darkness comprehended it not."*

No More Deception
The Devil's arrest has another specific purpose: God stops Satan from deceiving the nations. It is significant that the time of Satan's imprisonment is given: *"...a thousand years...."*

We know from Scripture that *"...one day is with the Lord as a thousand years, and a thousand years as one day."* No man ever lived a thousand years, because God said, *"...for in the day that thou eatest thereof thou shalt surely die"* (Genesis 2:17). Adam, to whom this warning was addressed, lived nine hundred and thirty years, seventy years short of a thousand!

During the Great Tribulation
After Satan is arrested and incapacitated, peace begins. We see a special category of saved people ruling with Jesus for a thousand years. This is a specific group of believers. They are identified as those who:

- Were beheaded for the witness of Jesus and for the Word of God;
- Have not worshiped the beast;
- Neither his image;
- Neither received the mark upon the forehead or in the hand.

These are the people that live and reign with Christ a thousand years! Obviously, there must be *other* people on Earth at that time over which these saints will rule with the Lord.

Where is the Church?

The Scriptures make it clear that the church, which is the body of Christ, will be raptured from the Earth before the Tribulation. From that moment on, we will remain in His presence. Our actual position is described in 1st Thessalonians 4:17, *"...and so shall we ever be with the Lord."* Therefore, wherever the Lord is, there we shall be also. When He returns to Earth and rules, we too will be part of it because we are His body. But the Bible does not clarify our function as the body of Christ while we are with the Lord on Earth.

The First Resurrection

Jesus is the first fruit from among the dead. He is the beginning of the first resurrection. The Rapture of the church is the finalizing of His resurrection. It is a demonstration of His absolute victory over death as it is written, *"...then shall be brought to pass the saying that is written, Death is swallowed up in victory. O death, where is thy sting? O grave, where is thy victory?"* (1st Corinthians 15:54–55). Prophetically speaking, however, the first resurrection continues, just as salvation in Jesus Christ continues after the Rapture.

Why is Satan Temporarily Paroled?

During the reign of Christ on Earth, the world will be filled with the knowledge of the Lord, according to Habakkuk 2:14, *"For the earth shall be filled with the knowledge of the glory of the LORD, as the waters cover the sea."* The deceiver is incapacitated and people will not be led astray. Thus, the logical question we need to ask is, "Why does God permit Satan to be loosed out of his prison?"

The result of his release is described in Revelation 20: 8–9, *"And shall go out to deceive the nations which are in the four quarters of the earth, Gog, and Magog, to gather them together to battle: the number of whom is as the sand of the sea. And they went up on the breadth of the earth, and compassed the camp of the saints about, and the beloved city: and fire came down from God out of heaven, and devoured them."*

Are we to assume that Satan will use his deceptive capabilities to again gather the nations, who then will arm themselves in order to make war against "the beloved city"? This is what the Scripture seems to indicate.

Since we now know in part only, we cannot fully recognize the events of the future that will take place more than a thousand years from now. However, it is my understanding that the "nations" mentioned here in verse 8 are the masses of fallen angels who have originally taken sides with Satan and not literal nations of human beings.

The conclusion I have drawn is presented to the church for judgment. I am fully aware that most, if not all, scholars of eschatology view the event described in Revelation 20 differently. But I have found it necessary to reanalyze various interpretations, and what I present here is not claimed to be the ultimate interpretation. But it seems a logical answer. Honest and open criticism of this interpretation is welcomed by the author.

Satan's Beginning

To better understand who these "nations" are, we will read Isaiah's description of the origin and the end of Satan, *"How art thou fallen from heaven, O Lucifer, son of the morning! how art thou cut down to the ground, which didst weaken the nations! For thou hast said in thine heart, I will ascend into heaven, I will exalt my throne above the stars of God: I will sit also upon the mount of the congregation, in the sides of the north:*

"I will ascend above the heights of the clouds; I will be like the most High. Yet thou shalt be brought down to hell, to the sides of the pit" (Isaiah 14:12–15). We must remember that

this statement is a prophecy of Satan's origin and his end. The fallen "nations," which are the fallen angels, are already in hell. They are powerless and they see Satan coming and ask the question, *"...are thou also become weak as we? Are thou become like unto us?"* (verse 10). Then in verse 12, they identify his position in relationship to the fallen angels, *"...how art thou cut down to the ground, which didst weaken the nations!"* (verse 12). Who are these nations? Quite obviously, the nations of fallen angels! Satan did not weaken the nations of the world. He is the god of the nations of this world. He strengthens the nations, *"...let the weak say I am strong"* (Joel 3:10).

In Jude, we read of the angels who followed Satan: *"And the angels which kept not their first estate, but left their own habitation, he hath reserved in everlasting chains under darkness unto the judgment of the great day"* (Verse 6).

The Stars of Heaven—What They Are
Revelation 12:4 tells us that one-third of the stars of heaven were cast upon the Earth. This corresponds to Daniel 8:10 where he talks of the Antichrist: *"And it waxed great, even to the host of heaven; and it cast down some of the host and of the stars to the ground, and stamped upon them."*

What kind of "stars" is the Bible referring to here? Let's look at the origin of the Devil. Isaiah 14:12 reads, *"...O Lucifer, son of the morning...."* Luther translates this as, *"Thou beautiful star of the morning."* And the Hebrew Bible says, *"O shining One, Son of Dawn."* This clearly indicates that the Devil was once a glorious creation called the "star of the morning." Only the King James translation attaches a *name* to the star, Lucifer.

This fallen star named Lucifer took with him, at his fall, one-third of the heavenly angelic hosts. It is evident that these "stars" are not the stars we see in the night sky. We know that to be impossible because many of those stars we see with our eyes are significantly larger in size than planet Earth. Thus we know the "stars" the Bible is referring to are fallen angels.

Peter furthermore confirms that God's angels were cast down and reserved unto punishment, *"For if God spared not the angels that sinned, but cast them down to hell, and delivered them into chains of darkness, to be reserved unto judgment"* (2nd Peter 2:4).

Enduring Peace

The thousand-year kingdom of peace starts with mankind beating their swords into plowshares. The Bible indicates men will learn war no more.

The manufacturing of weapons is done away with. How, then, can men gather to battle? Isaiah 2:4 testifies, *"And he shall judge among the nations, and shall rebuke many people: and they shall beat their swords into plowshares, and their spears into pruninghooks: nation shall not lift up sword against nation, neither shall they learn war any more."* We emphasize here the words, "any more."

But there is another mighty reason: The guarantee of peace is subject to the universe, *"They* [all people] *shall fear thee* [God] *as long as the sun and moon endure, throughout all generations. He shall come down like rain upon the mown grass: as showers that water the earth. In his days shall the righteous flourish: and abundance of peace so long as the moon endureth"* (Psalm 72:5–7). Only when the sun and moon are done away with will this peace cease to exist!

The end of this last battle, the confrontation between the saints and the Devil, is described only briefly, *"...and fire came down from God out of heaven and devoured them."* No description of weapons, bodies, or machinery is found. We are given an additional method with which to identify these "nations."

Who are Gog and Magog?

What about the names, "Gog and Magog" in Revelation 20:8? Bible scholars agree that Gog and Magog of Ezekiel 38–39 is an area north of Israel—and today it is called Russia. What was unique about Russia was their attempt to dominate the world through communism. It is a fact that they were not antichristian, understanding that the description "antichrist" means "instead of Christ." Communism did not create a religion comparative to Christianity to deceive the nations, but they were outspoken and boldly anti-God!

Russian communism found its expression in hatred for religion. For over 70 years, they lifted up their fists against heaven and shouted, "There is no God!" and "God is dead!" But world communism, which is anti-God, has already received the first part of God's judgment: the Soviet Union's disintegration.

Another judgment is yet to follow based on the Scripture found in Ezekiel 38 and 39: Russia's doomed invasion of Israel will take care of the military aspect of "Gog and Magog," the symbol of anti-God! The Ezekiel 38–39 battle, often called the battle of Gog and Magog, is a purely military judgment upon this power bloc.

It is also evident from Ezekiel 38:9 and 12 that this northern confederacy invades the land of Israel for gain, *"Thou shalt ascend and come like a storm, thou shalt be like a cloud to cover the land, thou, and all thy bands, and many people with thee...*

"To take a spoil, and to take a prey; to turn thine hand upon the desolate places that are now inhabited, and upon the people that are gathered out of the nations, which have gotten cattle and goods, that dwell in the midst of the land."

We see an additional confirmation that Russia and her allies intend to gain materially based on the three questions Israel's Arab neighbors ask in protest of the attack: *"Sheba, and Dedan, and the merchants of Tarshish, with all the young lions thereof, shall say unto thee, Art thou come to take a spoil? hast thou gathered thy company to take a prey? to carry away silver and gold, to take away cattle and goods, to take a great spoil?"* (Ezekiel 38:13). This invasion is aimed at taking "goods."

Who Are Sheba, Dedan, and Tarshish?

Sheba was the son of Ramah, a son of Cush, and had settled somewhere on the shores of the Persian Gulf. The Bible also mentions the kingdom of Sheba, located geographically on today's map in the area of Yemen.

Dedan is identified as the son of Ramah, the son of Cush, in Genesis 10:7 and 1st Chronicles 1:9. Also, Dedan is the son of Jokshan, Abraham's son, which he had with Keturah according to Genesis 25:3 and 1st Chronicles 1:32. *Ungers Bible Dictionary* places the descendants on the Syrian borders near the territory of Edom, located in today's Jordan.

While Tarshish cannot be identified geographically, it appears several times in the Old Testament and it is mentioned in connection with ships, merchants, and trade from the Mediterranean to the Persian Gulf.

It seems almost natural that the rich Arab states, with the immense sources of energy, ask some very natural and yet frightening questions regarding the true intention of the northern confederacy.

This should suffice to show that the Gog and Magog of Ezekiel 38 and 39 concerns a geographically-identifiable area, including a group of allied kings designated by name.

Demonic Origin of Gog and Magog

When we read the name "Gog and Magog," in Revelation 20:8, we understand this to be a tangible description of the anti-God sentiment. This should show that "Gog and Magog" of Revelation 20 are only related to "Gog and Magog" of Ezekiel

38 and 39 because they symbolize the "anti-God" aspect. Still, someone may insist, "This speaks of Gog and Magog."

To explain this further, let us look at some examples, such as the casting down of Satan. When describing the once-glorious morning star, Lucifer, Ezekiel identifies him by comparison to the king of Tyrus, *"Son of man, take up a lamentation upon the king of Tyrus, and say unto him, Thus saith the Lord God"* (Ezekiel 28:12). Through the judgment pronounced on the king of Tyrus, the prophet Ezekiel describes the fall of Satan. It is quite obvious that the king of Tyrus was never in *"...Eden the garden of God..."* (Ezekiel 28:13). He never was *"...the anointed cherub..."* (Ezekiel 28:14) and he never *"...walked on the holy mountain of God,"* or *"...in the midst of the stones of fire"* (verse 14). When Ezekiel describes the fall of Satan, he only uses the king of Tyrus as an *example* for us.

Later in history, when our Lord Jesus said to Peter *"...Get thee behind me, Satan..."* (Mark 8:33), He certainly addressed Peter, but through him Jesus meant Satan. This was done because Peter rebuked Jesus' prophecy that He would be killed. Thus Satan was using Peter as his mouthpiece.

"Gog and Magog" of Revelation 20 is the description of the last rebellion against the living God and has no relationship to the battle of Gog and Magog of Ezekiel 38 and 39. This is the final act of the spirit of "Gog and Magog"—rebellion against God!

Satan's Final End
The casting out of Satan will take place in three phases:

First, at the Rapture, Satan will be cast out with his angels from heaven, *"And there was war in heaven: Michael and his angels fought against the dragon; and the dragon fought and his angels, And prevailed not; neither was their place found any more in heaven.*

"And the great dragon was cast out, that old serpent, called the Devil, and Satan, which deceiveth the whole world: he was cast out into the earth, and his angels were cast out with him" (Revelation 12:7–9). This is banishment from heaven. Never again will he have access to heaven to accuse the brethren before God day and night.

Second, Satan is arrested and imprisoned at the end of the Great Tribulation. This is the banishment from Earth.

Third, at the end of the thousand-year kingdom of peace, he shall be loosed for a short time, which God uses to finalize Satan's eternal position. This results in the banishment of his access to the saints and the holy city for eternity.

Climax of Deception

We can barely imagine the horrible deception that will commence when Satan and his angels are cast out of heaven to Earth. He will be roaming this planet unhindered because the "light of the world," which dwells in the church, will be gone.

In addition, the bottomless pit is going to be opened and more devils will come out to torment mankind: *"And he opened the bottomless pit; and there arose a smoke out of the pit, as the smoke of a great furnace; and the sun and the air were darkened by reason of the smoke of the pit. And there came out of the smoke locusts upon the earth: and unto them was given power, as the scorpions of the earth have power"* (Revelation 9:2–3). These "locusts" are part of the underworld coming out of the bottomless pit, being members of the Devil's army. Therefore, we can understand why Jesus and the prophets spoke of this time as the most terrible time on Earth. Revelation 12:12 heralds the contrast: *"Therefore rejoice, ye heavens, and ye that dwell in them. Woe to the inhabiters of the earth and of the sea! for the devil is come down unto you, having great wrath, because he knoweth that he hath but a short time."*

The Name or the Number of the Beast

If life on Earth is impossible, seeing that those who refuse to worship the image will be killed and existence is virtually out of the question without the mark of the beast or the number of his name, who then is left but the remnant of Israel? Scriptures make it clear that nations will exist after the Great Tribulation and the gentiles will come and worship in Jerusalem.

It is also evident that our Lord is going to rule the nations with an iron rod from Jerusalem, *"And she brought forth a man child, who was to rule all nations with a rod of iron: and her child was caught up unto God, and to his throne"* (Revelation 12:5). If there are no nations left, how can this prophecy be fulfilled?

What about Moses' prophecy? *"For the LORD thy God blesseth thee, as he promised thee: and thou shalt lend unto many nations, but thou shalt not borrow; and thou shalt reign over many nations, but they shall not reign over thee"* (Deuteronomy 15:6). If there are no nations left, how shall Israel rule over them?

The Mark of the Beast

I propose, therefore, that we take another look at Revelation 13:15–17: *"And he had power to give life unto the image of the beast, that the image of the beast should both speak, and cause that as many as would not worship the image of the beast should be killed. And he causeth all, both small and great, rich and poor, free and bond, to receive a mark in their right hand, or in their foreheads:*

"And that no man might buy or sell, save he that had the mark, or the name of the beast, or the number of his name."

Death, therefore, is caused in the first place not by the Antichrist or the false prophet, but by the *image* of the beast. It is the *image* that executes the death sentence upon a non-worshiper, *"...that the image of the beast should both speak and cause that as many as would not worship the image of the beast should be killed"* (Revelation 13:15).

Verse 16 makes it plain that there are no exceptions: All people on Earth will be required to receive *"...a mark in their right hand or in their foreheads...."*

Dr. Wim Malgo, the founder of Midnight Call Ministry, interpreted this to mean that those who receive it in their right hand are the manual workers, and in the forehead, the intellectuals. Whether this is so, only time will tell. Verse 17 clearly explains that it will be impossible for anyone to survive: *"...save he that had the mark, or the name of the beast, or the number of his name."*

Two Different Marks

After having searched extensively through many translations, I have come to the conclusion that "the mark of the beast" consists of primarily two categories. From the best sources I have studied, it should read: "...save he that had the mark, which is the name of the beast or the number of his name." Therefore, we should deal with two categories: Those who receive the *mark* of the beast; and those who receive the *number* of his name.

Having established this fact, we must now determine what will happen to these two categories of people. What does the Bible say? When reading the entire book of Revelation, we notice that *the mark of the beast* is mentioned five times.

Three times it talks of eternal punishment and two times about the victory over the mark of the beast.

- *"And the smoke of their torment ascendeth up for ever and ever: and they have no rest day nor night, who worship the beast and his image, and whosoever receiveth **the mark** of his name"* (Revelation 14:11). This is plain: Eternal punishment "for ever and ever" for those who worship the image of the beast and those who receive the mark of his name.

- *"And the first went, and poured out his vial upon the earth; and there fell a noisome and grievous sore upon the men which had **the mark** of the beast, and upon them which worshipped his image"* (Revelation 16:2). Again, torment for those who have taken the mark of the beast and worshiped his image.

- *"And the beast was taken, and with him the false prophet that wrought miracles before him, with which he deceived them that had received **the mark** of the beast, and them that worshipped his image. These both were cast alive into a lake of fire burning with brimstone"* (Revelation 19:20). Once more, we see the image worshiper who received the mark of the beast.

- In Revelation 15:2, we read of the victors: *"And I saw as it were a sea of glass mingled with fire: and them that had gotten the victory over the beast, and over his image, and over **his mark**, and over the number of his name, stand on the sea of glass, having the harps of God."* Their victory is: 1) over the beast, 2) over the image, 3) over his mark, and 4) over the number of his name. Here we see a very special group of believers who have come out of the Great Tribulation.

- Lastly, Revelation 20:4 reads, *"And I saw thrones, and they sat upon them, and judgment was given unto them: and I saw the souls of them that were beheaded for the witness of Jesus, and for the word of God, and which had not worshipped the beast, neither his image, neither had received **his mark** upon their foreheads, or in their hands; and they lived and reigned with Christ a thousand years."*

What we learn from these five verses is that those who are condemned for ever and ever have received 1) the mark of the beast and 2) worshiped the image. We do not read, however, that those who have accepted "the *number* of his name" are in the same category of the condemned. Nevertheless, they will not belong to the ones who sing, in victory, the song of Moses and the song of the Lamb (Revelation 15:3).

I, therefore, propose that the ones who receive the *number* of his name will enter the millennial kingdom of peace. That fact, however, does not mean they are saved. Jesus will rule with a rod of iron and sinners will die during the millennium for their sins.

It is my understanding from the Scripture that a great multitude will not worship the image neither receive the mark of the beast, but will take the *number* of his name in order to survive. But they are still sinners and are in need of redemption.

Man, in his unregenerate state, is still corrupt through and through. But sin will no longer be tolerated during the millennial reign of Christ. It is quite obvious that those who enter the kingdom are still capable of committing sin. Thus we read in Isaiah 65:20: *"There shall be no more thence an infant of days, nor an old man that hath not filled his days: for the child shall die an hundred years old; but the sinner being an hundred years old shall be accursed."* The last sentence in the Hebrew Bible reads, *"And he who fails to reach a hundred shall be reckoned accursed."* I repeat, entering the millennium does not mean the person is saved. Sinners will die and *"...shall be accursed."* When the thousand years are completed, there will be no more sinners on Earth, only saints!

I am fully aware that this interpretation is new but I felt impressed to present it to the church and let it judge based on the Word of God. According to my understanding, this is the only way to have literal nations living on Earth besides the Jews in the millennium.

Conclusion

Let me emphasize strongly that there is no salvation outside of Jesus Christ. Only He was able to pay, with His own blood, the required penalty for the sins of all mankind. Only in His name can we be saved. Only through Jesus can we come to God.

Throughout the writing of this book, I have emphasized that our hope lies in trusting Him, not in manmade religion, or democracy. I believe that the danger of trusting in democracy has been thoroughly exposed.

If I had presented the premise that communism would lead to the establishment of the Antichrist, most would have agreed without hesitation. The same holds true for dictatorships or other forms of government which restrict our freedom and rules over us without our vote. But democracy in our minds equals freedom, and we love and trust it. How ironic that what we love, trust and desire as human beings is the exact catalyst which will bring God and man on a collision course and subsequent final judgment.

Dear reader, the Bible says, *"...now is the accepted time; behold, now is the day of salvation"* (2nd Corinthians 6:2). If you are not a child of God today, simply confess your sins and acknowledge that you are unable to save yourself. Ask Jesus to come into your heart and thank Him that He has promised in His own Word, *"And it shall come to pass, that whosoever shall call on the name of the Lord shall be saved"* (Acts 2:21).

Absolute eternal bliss is awaiting those who are saved and absolute eternal damnation for those who are lost. You must make a decision. Where will you spend eternity?

ENDNOTES

Chapter 2
1 Reuters, 1/24/94
2 Dispatch From Jerusalem, 12/94, p.2
3 The State, 12/25/94, p.D-1

Chapter 3
4 The Scotsman, 1/3/94
5 U.S.News, 11/8/93
6 Jerusalem Post Intl. Edition, 6/17/95, p.4

Chapter 4
7 Jerusalem Post, 1/28/95, p.4
8 Outpost, April 1994, p.5
9 Outpost, April 1994, p.5
10 Jerusalem Post, 1/28/95, p.3
11 Dispatch From Jerusalem, 12/93, p.8

Chapter 6
12 U.S.News 12/20/93 (Cover story)
13 The Scotsman, 5/28/94

Chapter 7
14 Newsweek, 5/30/94, p.68
15 The News and Observer, 2/9/95

Chapter 8
16 The State, 3/19/94, p.D8
17 Global Peace/Rise of Antichrist, p.129
18 Far Eastern Econ. Rev. 2/2/95, p.52

Chapter 9
19 Wire reports, 11/26/93
20 Popular Science, 1/94
21 Daily Mail, 4/2/94
22 Reuters, 12/29/93
23 Christians and Israel, V.3/No.1, p.5
24 Kansas City Star, 1/15/95
25 The Herald, 4/4/94

Chapter 10
26 The State, 12/12/94
27 The European, 3/9/95
28 Courier Journal, 5/11/84, p.A7
29 The Voice, Diocese of Newark, 1/89
30 L'Observatore Romano, 2/10/86, p.5
31 The European, 12/15/94, p.1
32 The European, 5/26/94, p.25
33 The State, 12/3/93

Chapter 11
34 The State, 7/6/95, p.B10

Chapter 12
35 The European, 7/6/95, p.17

Chapter 13
36 *Know the Marks of Cults*, Dave Breese

Chapter 15
37 Kansas City Star, 4/26/92
38 Feer Herzog, Swiss Finance Minister, 1870

Chapter 16
39 The Futurist, 1-2/95, p.14–17

Chapter 17
40 News From Israel, 7/89

Chapter 18
41 Midnight Call, 5/95, p.24
42 Reuters, 12/29/93

Chapter 20
43 Catholic Register, 9/74

➡ *Tap into the Bible analysis of top prophecy authorities...*

Midnight Call is a hard-hitting Bible-based magazine loaded with news, commentary, special features, and teaching, illustrated with explosive color pictures and graphics. Join hundreds of thousands of readers in 140 countries who enjoy this magazine regularly!

➡ *The world's leading prophetic Bible magazine*

➡ *Covering international topics with detailed commentary*

➡ *Bold, uncompromising Biblical stands on issues*

➡ *Pro-family, Pro-life, Pro-Bible*

12 issues/1 yr. $28.95
24 issues/2 yr. $45